THE
BATTLE
FOR THE SOUL
OF NIGER-DELTA

VICTOR DENILA

THE POLITICAL MAP OF NIGERIA

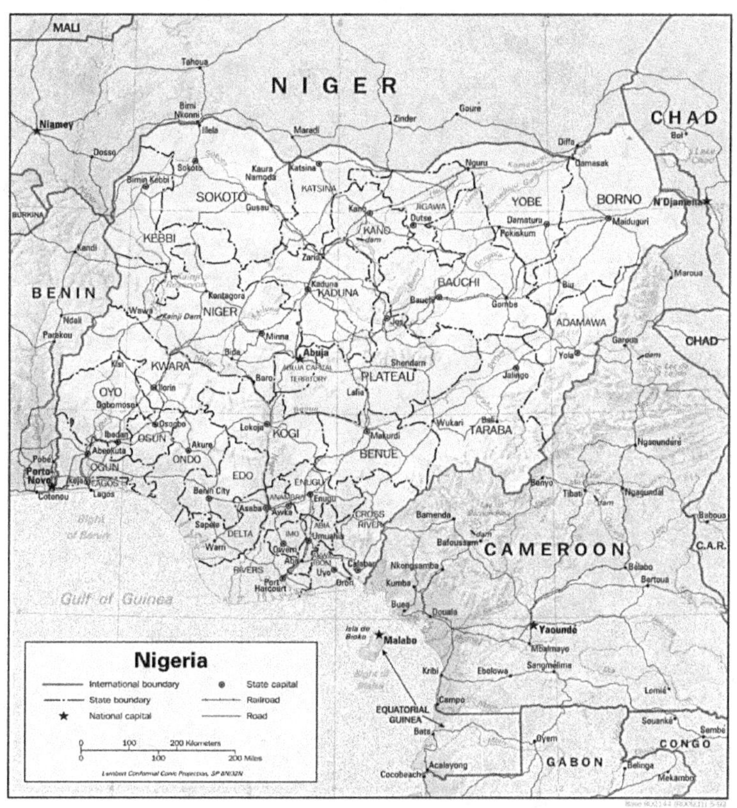

THE BATTLE FOR THE SOUL OF NIGER-DELTA

VICTOR

DENILA

Published by: **SOUL PLANE MULTIMEDIA LTD**
No 10, Oyelola Street, Anifowoshe, Ikeja, Lagos
Email: soul_plane_ml@yahoo.com
TEL: 08020769855, 07031805642

ACKNOWLEDGEMENTS

This is to acknowledge the contributions of the following persons and corporate bodies to the success of this book. First, the contributions of ThisDay, the Guardian, and the Vanguard newspapers have been immense in the inspiration of this book. Their contribution to the issues of resource control and SNC struggle is worth commending.

The effort of the former Delta State governor Chief James Ibori and the Akwa Ibom State former governor are also inspirational in the writing of this book. They gave vent to the belief of the ordinary citizens of the region the course to liberate the Niger Delta and indeed the Nigeria masses. Professor Itse Sagay, Chief Edwin Clark, Hon. Temi Harriman are worth commending for their effort and struggle. They are inspirational.

My respect also goes to the dead heroes who had given their lives for this course. Kenule Saro-Wiwa, Isaac Adaka Boro, Alhaja Kudirat Abiola and many others who have died to make the truth inevitable within the nation polity. Posterity will never forget the contributions of all, both living and dead. They are indeed the true heroes of the nation, the true nationalists.

Thanks also to the following people, Mr. Joshua Denila, for his role and support in this project and also for the poems he contributed. His financial and moral support is also acknowledged. Mrs. Elizabeth Messiri who has never doubted a brother's ability and talent, she is indeed one in a million. Eng. Tata Messiri for being supportive. To all of you, I say I am grateful.

I thank all my friends who one way or the other contributed to make this project a reality. Adebayo

Otenaike, and so many others too numerous to mention, I say thanks to all of you.

I thank Mr. Kenneth Ilalokhoin, who despite his tight schedules went through this book and made necessary corrections. I thank my mum who against all odds stood me, my mother-in-law for her unwavering faith in my ability and last but not the least; I thank, Mrs Christabel Denila for her support throughout this project. She has been quite inspirational. Above all things, God Almighty, the source of inspiration is greatly thanked for life and inspiration.

VICTOR DENILA

DEDICATION

This book is dedicated to all the heroes (organisations and individuals) of Resource Control and Sovereign National Conference both living and dead. They are the true heroes of a future Nigeria emanating from the shambles of a squandered legacy.

FOREWORD

INTRODUCTION

The former Nigeria President, Chief Olusegun Obasanjo, in November 2001 set up a Special Security Committee. The committee has as its head the then Chief of Army Staff, Rtd. Lt. Gen. Alex Ogomudia. It also had as members, other security chiefs from the other security outfits. The committee among other things has as a point of reference:

- To look into prevailing situation in the oil producing areas which have in recent past witnessed unprecedented vandalisation of oil pipelines, disruptions, kidnappings, extortion, and a general state of insecurity.

When the committee finished its sittings, it made the following observations:

- Causes of insecurity in the oil producing areas have to do with the neglect, frustration, and sense of abandonment shared by the people.
- It also stated that enduring peace cannot be achieved by militarization or security approach.

In recommending solution, the committee made the following recommendations:

- Payment of not less than 50% derivation to the oil producing areas.
- Increase in local content by oil companies.

- Repeal land use act, petroleum act, and all laws dispossessing the people of their God-given wealth.

The committee however failed to tell the president that the people even need to know why they should be Nigerians and what their contribution to being Nigerians should be. In that line of duty, the committee failed. Is the general state of insecurity that is engulfing the nation just a Niger Delta affair? What about the other parts of the country where one cannot feel free as a Nigerian?

Is it just a question of granting 50% derivation to the producers of any mineral resources and then go to sleep expecting that all is well? What is wrong with the Nigerian nation? Why have we not been able to build a strong and united nation after almost hundred years of coexisting as a nation? Is the present configuration of the Nigerian state on right foundation? These are the questions that the nation needs to answer. The believe that we need to have or practice true federalism is fast gaining ground in the South while the North sees that agitation as unpatriotic. So what do we do? Perhaps we should review the basis of our coexistence as a nation with the view to strengthening our unity.

Despite the myriads of recommendations and white papers written and submitted to the federal government at resolving the problems within the Niger Delta, the spot remains a hot bed of crises. The problems within the area have defied solution and the government has also failed to implement the several recommendations made to it especially those that have direct bear on resource control.

The entire nation has sat down aloof and watch the Niger Delta suffer the pains and agony of neglect to the favour of other regions. This is fast becoming a problem to the entire nation. The problems seem insurmountable and the nation seems to reap the benefits of the crises within the region.

The nation needs to talk. The people need to negotiate. This book examines the basis of the existence of the Nigeria State as a nation and traces the root of the present problems. It examines the basis of our coexistence as a nation and the conspiracy and falsehood upon which the nation had been built. It justifies the resource control agitation as well as the call for sovereign national conference. It also delves into the corruption of the leaders as well as the multinational oil companies.

I find this an interesting reading for those who must understand why we agitate for resource control and the Sovereign National Conference. The aim of this book is to present in the simplest form, reasons for these agitation and why they are necessary presently in order to save the future of this country and make all equal in the pursuit of progress for the nation.

PART ONE

NIGERIA: POLITICS OF NATIONALITIES BEFORE AND AFTER AMALGAMATION

- THE PRE-COLONIAL NATIONALITIES
- THE SUPPRESSION AND AMALGAMATION

CHAPTER ONE

<u>NIGERIA'S ETHNIC NATIONALITIES AND THE NIGER DELTA</u>

In reference to Professor Otite Onigu; there are five characteristics of ethnic nationalities derived from a combination of political sociology and anthropology. These are:

1). Share in a common culture and identity, language, history and kinship; this is also called complimentarity of communication.
2). Encapsulation of the full range of demographic division of age and gender and a network of economic, political and social institutions.
3). A differentiation in wealth, status and power.
4). Homeland or home territory for an ethnic group.
5). Members of ethnic nationalities share coexistence with other group outside the homeland.

A former Nigeria military president, General Ibrahim Badamosi Babangida, speaking on 'Challenges of Governance in a Plural Nigeria' opined that using the above computations Nigeria has 389 ethnic groups. In my days in the secondary school, I am sure it is still the same view; it was taught that Nigeria has 250 ethnic nationalities.

The former leader went ahead to give the figures as Adamawa 80 groups, Bauchi 50, Plateau 52, Taraba 32, Cross River 30, Nassarawa 25, Niger 22, Borno 23 and Kebbi 19. Other states range from between 4 in Kwara and Bayelsa and 17 in Gombe State.

Nigeria as a nation is thus made up of three hundred and eighty nine ethnic nationalities coexisting as a plural state brought about by the forces of colonial coercion. The road to our coexistence began with the ambition of the colonial authorities and in disrespect to the history of the people to be so brought together, decided that we must live together for good or bad. The colonial masters did not see the new state or its people as a people deserving of their respect but as a conquered people who must obey and respect her wish. Motives for nation building were thus geared towards the development of their home country in this regard; United Kingdom and the Nigeria State and other conquered African countries must become the milk that feeds the home country and its industries.

Further abuse of a people sovereign right was the amalgamation in 1914 of the North and Southern part of Nigeria by Lord Lugard. This was not done because the component units so wished to be lumped together as one but because the British felt running two countries was cumbersome. The North was administratively not viable for the colonialist to run. It was cheaper to run a single country for the colonialists. The country was governed like a conquered territory not like a country of people that had through the years evolved their own history.

Today's Nigeria stands on trio-ethnic tripod, an arrangement that completely ignores the existence of other ethnic groups despite the fact that some of these other minor groups predate them. Politics in Nigeria is tilted in favour of these three ethnic groups precluding

16

others from even thinking of being part of the union. The Hausas, the Yorubas and the Ibos, three ethnic groups which have so much undermine the coexistence of this nation are perhaps kept together, or united in one common goal. That goal as it would seem is the battle for the soul of the Niger Delta. Other Northern minorities who have seen themselves as part of the move to perpetually enslave and plunder the Niger Delta have joined these retrogressive forces.

The Niger Delta has become the sweet bride whose cancerous breasts feeds the nation but must bear the anguish of the cancer infested breast all alone. Thus, while the others feed and get healthier, the Niger Delta is left devastated and plundered. To make sure that the plunder goes on unabated, the people are deliberately set up against one another politically, in bid to forestall the unity that would lead to total emancipation of the region within the Nigeria polity.

The British seem to have consciously negotiated with the other groups to perpetually keep the people who once ran kingdoms that predated the rest of the country in civilization under political control. The control and the domination of the people of the Niger Delta area by outsiders is a task that the indigenous population has risen against in recent times. This is against the backdrop of the harsh environment occasioned by the nefarious activities of crude oil explorations.

Today's Nigeria is obviously not the arrangement of the component units and it is a contraption that more strength has gone into keeping together as one than the people actually living together as one people with one another. Nigeria's attainment of independence has seemed more like throwing two antagonists into a secluded arena without clear definition of their powers and proper territorial delimitation. It is the answer to this question of ethnic rights and limitations that the entire nation seems to have been searching for more than fifty years after independence.

There is a popular saying that if you do not know where you are headed, then it is better to head back to where your journey began. Perhaps from there you can begin to refocus and find a new destination that might hold greater promise. So where is Nigeria headed? In the first place where did Nigeria as a nation even begin?

Pre-colonial Nigeria though provides us with an insight into what might have happened if Nigeria had evolved on her own as a nation without the hands of the colonialists. These are to be examined in the next discourse.

PRE-COLONIAL NIGERIA

History is replete with so many ethnic heroes who had gone on conquest missions and had absorbed smaller unit of ethnic group into the more powerful and more organized states/kingdom. As this happened, the conquered group was either completely absorbed into the new kingdom to become a subgroup of the kingdom in language, art and culture or simply fought to retain its identity but submissive to the more powerful kingdom. In some other cases, these heroes left the powerful kingdom and went to found new states, independent of the home state.

These we see in the adventures of Oduduwa, (Izoduwa) the Benin prince who founded the modern obaship at Ile-Ife and his son Oranmiyan whom he sent to Benin to go and rule in his stead but rather than rule founded the Benin dynasty and went on to establish the great Oyo Empire. By the time Oyo Empire was being

18

established as an empire, Benin was in the second phase of her political history translating from the rule of the Ogisos to the Obas. Tsoede established the Nupe kingdom after a political misadventure in the land of the Igalas. Bayagida as well as queen Amina was immortal heroes of the Hausa fame. The Kanem-Borno Empire had one of the most formidable political histories in the Sudan.

By the time most kingdoms were finding their roots, Benin had discarded the more authoritarian rule of the 'Ogisos' to a more definite monarchical form of government. By the time other kingdoms were taking roots, Benin had begun to receive visitors from the land of the whites. Benin went on to become one of the most formidable rain-forest states in the entire sub-Sahara Africa in politics and economy. The empire controlled a greater part of the regions under the present Western Nigeria. Most of the states that are today claiming Omo Oduduwa were actually parts of the old Benin Empire.

It is important to state here that despite the fact the leadership of most Yoruba states and the Benin dynasty were from the same source – the Benin prince called Izoduwa (Oduduwa) yet, Oduduwa even when the Benins asked him to come back home from exile to come and rule did not embark on uniting Ile-Ife with Benin as one kingdom. Rather, he sent his son Oranmiyan to go and rule Benin in his stead.

The Oyo Empire itself extended to parts of today's Republic of Benin at its height making military incursions into some of the earlier portions of Benin land, especially those at the boarder fringes with the empire like the Ekiti states, the Ijebus and much later Lagos. At the later periods, political boundaries between the Binis and the Oyos began to readjust itself as well as the boundaries between the Binis and the Igalas who were lords on the other side of the Niger. So was the commercial city of Onitsha lost as it kept intermingling with the Ibo elements of the East?

The Nupes who had established themselves also began to lose some of their territories to the incursion of the jihadists in the North. The entire Hausa states fell to the jihadists as well as the Jukun State. The only kingdom in the North that survived and repelled the incursion of the jihadists was the Kanem-Borno Empire. Thus, Borno was never part of the caliphate that came to be established in the early nineteenth century. Various emirates were established in the North by the jihadists whose incursions into the forest states were greatly repelled by the Yorubas after the sack of the old Oyo Empire at Igboho. Their ambition to bring Islam and establish a caliphate over the entire area that is today known as Nigeria was also greatly repelled by the Benin warriors who fought to the North of the kingdom to preserve their heritage. The coming of the Europeans also contributed to the halting of the jihadists' ambition of Islamic crusade.

It should be noted that if the Europeans had not stopped or intervened in the nascent states re-emerging from various civil wars from the kingdoms and the Jihadists ambitions; two possible scenarios would have emerged in the evolution of the country called Nigeria today. First of all we should examine the factors that have made these languages, Hausa, Ibo and Yoruba the most widely spoken languages in the Nigeria of today as against Bini, Igala, Nupe and Ijaw. That Yoruba is one of the most widely spoken languages in Nigeria today is due to the fact that Oyo Empire, the actual root of the Yoruba language was a restless kingdom of adventurous warriors.

The Oyo Empire made so many military incursions into most of the Yoruba-speaking areas of

20

today which had hitherto been under the control of the Benin Empire like the Ondo areas, the Lagos area and the Ijebu area. Through trade and social interactions these became Yorubas as new wave of migrations from the old sites joined the inhabitants. As these migrations occurred, the original identities of these people became lost. Much the same conditions applied to the Ibo-speaking areas of Onitsha, Asaba, Agbor etc.

That Ibo is today widely spoken in the Eastern part of Nigeria had nothing to do with the military conquest of any of the areas which is today Iboland. Neither has it anything to do with a common ancestry of the people. The Ibos from Onitsha came from Benin and so were most of the Western Ibos. Oguta people came from Benin. Some others especially around the north of Anambra and Enugu came from the Igalaland. Commodity trade and slave trade made the language a more acceptable one among the other smaller tribes.

Hausa became the acceptable language and more so a second language to most other Northerners as the jihadists made great incursions into the middle belt. These jihadists replaced the natural rulers in most palaces establishing themselves as rulers and teachers of the new faith. It is a wonder that the jihadists spoke Hausa as against Fulbe, the language of the Fulanis who were the arrowheads of the Jihad. As the people embraced Islam so they embraced the Hausa language, the language of their new overlords. The basis for expansion in the North as against that of the South was religious and political rather than the usual economic and political dominance. It is often a widely held belief among the founders of the new faith that through political power, every other thing can be changed. So they were not just coming to change the religion, they came to establish their political dominance.

The jihadists were only interested in Islamizing the entire country. They took Ilorin from the Yorubas and sacked Igboho, the headquarters of Oyo Empire. The action of the jihadists is responsible for the large number of Muslims among the Yoruba tribe today. Further South, the Itshekiri language became a variant of the Yoruba language as they interacted through the waters with the Ilajes who themselves spoke another variant of Yoruba.

The Ijaws due to the peculiar nature of their environment experienced little interactions with the upland people except with Urhobo, Itshekiri and Ibo elements. These had little influence on the language of the people, as these other tribes did not mingle much through intermarriage and settlement with them. On the basis of tongue, a Nigeria that would have evolved definitely would not have a single tongue for the people dwelling therein but a federation of multi-lingua nation. If the jihadists had succeeded then we would have been one Islamic nation with Hausa as the official language of the country.

The pre-colonial Nigeria was taking shape before the European incursions as a result of their own greed. The European powers were battle ready against each other as to who controls the trade from most of trade routes in Africa. The Yoruba civil wars, the decline of the Benin empire, the decline of Kanem –Borno empire, the diminishing powers of the Igalas, the emerging power of the jihadists, the increasing awareness among the Ibos of their collective existence. All these would have somehow contributed to building a nation or several nations out of the present structure called Nigeria.

Africa was denied the potential of the full evolution of its history by the Europeans who came to disrupt a natural process of evolution. Crisis is a normal process of evolution in the lives of nations and even in
22

the life of an individual. These crises go to mould the character of the individual or the nation that so evolved. The Roman Empire for example had fallen and risen several times to become the modern day Europe. The crises in the US that led to the civil war in the nineteenth century made her a stronger nation. The English who themselves became masters in colonialism had undergone so much crises in their history.

It should be noted that despite being part of the old Roman Empire most of the European nations of today had become nations along ethnic lines dictated by common history. The Germans, the French, the Poles, Swedish etc all were nations based on common history, ethnic affinity and language. Ireland is today not part of the United Kingdom because the two had no common history or ancestry. Where these were achieved by the use of force, the result had been unprecedented crises like Yugoslavia, Czechoslovakia etc.

The fate of the Union of Soviet Socialist Republic is another example of historical contraption. The USSR state today has collapsed along ethnic lines as compulsion rather than negotiation brought the nationalities together. Today we have as many tribes as formed the old Union as independent nations. This is because the communist revolution of 1917 in the old Russia coerced the other ethnic nationalities into the Union using brutal force. The system has thus collapsed beyond what could be salvaged. Perhaps, the agitation in today Nigeria would not be so vehement if the nation had evolved on its own through its natural history.

In the pre-colonial Benin Empire, it was the choice of the people that they desire a new king from Ife. In most of the weak kingdoms, in the time of crisis it was often the choice of the people to seek protection treaties with powerful kings. These treaties usually did not make them entirely dependent on the king. The treaties usually preserved their autonomy while paying tribute tax to the bigger king. This was the kind of treaty that was between Akure and Benin. The people were allowed to operate their own system. This was also the case between the Edos and the Itshekiris, the Igalas and the Jukuns, the Nupes and the Igalas, the Oyos and the Dahomeys.

In situations where the central power exploits the weakness of the smaller units of the kingdom and become too greedy or begin to overexert the smaller community, the people who are subjects revolt. They then begin to assert their own sovereignty over their land, especially where they had noticed the weaknesses in the system. This happened when the Itshekiris, the Akures, the Ishans revolted against the Benin sovereignty during the reign of Ovoramwen.

From the early nineteenth century, there was great revolt and wars in the present day Nigeria. These wars were mostly fought along ethnic lines as every ethnic group began to assert themselves over their land. The great kingdoms had become weak and new powers were about emerging from the ruins of the war and the open trade with the Europeans. The Yoruba civil war for instance would have seen to the emergence of new ethnic powers, which eventually could have ended in a confederation for not producing a single super power like the old Oyo Empire which, had virtually collapsed. The Egbas fought as a group, the Ijebus defended their homeland, the Ekitis fought as an independent group, the Shakis, the Ibadans had established a new homeland independent of Oyo, and the Dahomeys had gained their independence. These all fought to assert themselves as new powers independent of a declining centre at Oyo.

As these fought it should be noted that they began to assert themselves, they had also developed dialects distinct from the original Yoruba. Thus we have an Ibadan dialect of Yoruba, the Egba also distinct as well as the Ekitis. In the Benin Empire, this trend is also noticed in the Agbor language and dialect which is distinct from other Ibos as well as the Ukwanis all of whom were original Benin migrants. In the same vein, the North through jihad had become monolithic in language as Hausa had become a second language in all the conquered territories.

In the East, it was a case of communal living among the Ibos, the Ijaws and the Kalabaris. No group dominated the other politically or economically. Each community respected the right of the other community to exist as autonomous community. This communal and republican nature of the Ibos was destroyed by the colonialists who came to impose community leaders in the manner of the old kingdoms of Oyo and Benin and the style of the feudalistic North on the people. This is still a problem till today among the Ibos who have begun to see the new life style as a means of class distinction. The average Ibo man wants to become a king even if it is in a street, a culture alien to the tribe.

Africans from history had always become part of each other through military pacts as it was emerging in the Yoruba civil war, or military conquest as could be seen in the expeditions of the bigger empires or through democratic pacts as it was seen in the Ibo republican system. Nigeria would have emerged as a fully evolved nation that had on its own undergone historical changes through ethnic accords and pacts. This would have meant either a single nation with regional or ethnic autonomy or several nations formed along historical, religious or language affinity.

The Nigeria of today is one that had not been allowed the kind of evolution that the rest of Europe had undergone. Today's Europe is a composition of countries that had been formed along ethnic lines. So the problem of ethnicity is not peculiar to Africa. The Europeans enjoyed the full evolution of their political and economic system without much interruption from the outside. Europe would have been a single nation under the Romans, the Germans, the French or the Soviets if certain ambitions had not been halted when muted, like the ambitions of Napoleon, Hitler, Musolini and the Joseph Stanlin.

The Romans ruled Europe through the Holy Roman Empire. This collapsed as the nations freed themselves of this hold. Then came the French through Napoleon Bonaparte who went on military expeditions against the rest of Europe. He was resisted as the others asserted their ethnic independence. After him came the Germans, before the Germans, the Russians had begun to annex the rest of Eastern Europe through Marxist ideological campaigns. The communists' movements were non-negotiable. Every conquered territory became part of the Soviet Union. The Soviet Union is of course history, about ninety years after. The adventure of the Germans through Hitler was halted by a combination of the might of the rest nationalities.

The entire Europe of today was the remnant of the old Roman Empire that collapsed as each of the ethnic nationals began to assert their independence. Other attempts at resurrecting the kingdom forcefully had met with great resistance from all the units that made up today's Europe. Modern attempt at achieving what military actions could not achieve is now being done through the institution of the European Union, a body negotiating the coming together of Europe as a nation. These were the same people that came to force the unwilling Africans to be lumped together for their own

26

economic interest. It should be noted that when their interests began to clash in the region, the Western powers went on to negotiate African territories for themselves leaving out the Africans, whose territory was appropriated.

The pre-colonial Nigeria presented an interesting study that probably would have developed into one whole, evolving by itself, rather than by deliberate tinkering from the colonial masters. The options are that modern Nigeria would have been made up of several independent nations. Or a bigger whole that would have evolved by negotiation after a turbulent war of ethnic nationalities as was being witnessed in the old Oyo Empire, the declining Benin Kingdom, the Lagos impasse, the republican nature of the Ibos and the aggressive nature of the jihadists.

The implications are that we could either have an Islamic nation as the ambition of the jihadists would have dictated or a fragmented nation along ethnic nationalities as the ambitions of the natural leaders would have demanded. Better still, there could have been a better Nigeria in the present configuration evolving from the negotiating table of a confab of ethnic nationalities. The last option would have produced a better nation with true justice, peace, security and equity.

Given the last scenario, any political entity coming out would have been by negotiations. If however on the other hand an Islamic nation had emerged through the jihad, we would have sat down as robots to be manipulated by the whims and caprices of the gluttonous leaders, brainwashed by religious schisms that gives us no right to question the acts of our leaders. Then we would expect liberation like was the case with Turkey through the intervention of the five majors. Perhaps, under the hold of religion, Nigeria would have been more united, this is only an assumption.

None of the above situations had been allowed to take place. The colonialists came and cut short the ambition of the jihadists, suppressed the civil war of independence in the Yoruba states, quench the fire of Benin fury that Ovoramwen was rekindling, brought dubious treaties to unsuspecting, uneducated African leaders. They found willing tools in the hands of rulers who were more interested in keeping their feudalistic lordship. They compelled the resisting leader through the powers of the gun.

If Nigeria had emerged without British tinkering, the minimal obtainable system would have been the ethnic nationalities asserting themselves politically and economically. And for the fear of being annexed, each nationality would have developed its potential politically and economically in areas of superior advantage as we saw in post colonial Nigeria trades. While the North was the trade route for hides and skin to the North Africa, the Benin kingdom was noted for bronze casting, while salt production was the exclusive preserve of the Tivs and the tribes around the Benue and Niger rivers. The Ijaws were the fishermen; palm oil market was for the Ibos and the Urhobos.

If not through conquest by war and assimilation of conquered territories both culturally and economically, it should have been expected therefore that these political entities that ran their political and economic institutions independent of each other should have sat down at a conference to decide to live together than be compelled to live together as the British had done through coercion. Such decision would have set out conditions of coexistence. It would have ensured our unity rather than the disparity currently noticed in the British contraption

28

made possible through dubious treaties and conquest of the component units.

It is thus arguable what Nigeria should look like or arguable that the current federating units were members of the union not by choice but by compulsion. So there is need for restructuring of the system. This compulsion has impoverished the nation rather than enriches it. The Britons have left the nation in the hands of further plunderers of the nation to enable them continue the plunder and colonialism through imperialism. The old political order of pre-colonial Nigeria had good checks and balances in every community, which has now been corrupted in the new order. The discovery of free wealth in oil has increased the inordinate desire of the average Nigerian to be corrupt.

The hold on the nation has been dictated by this wealth which has made all leaders since independence to look away from the inherent problems in the configuration of Nigeria and address the problem as should be. They would rather greedily promote falsehood in the old tune of unity when none actually exists but among the rulers. Their desire to serve the nation is only equated with their desire to enrich themselves with the wealth so freely given to the detriment of the natural environment and future of the nation.

Heroism and patriotism has been thrown to the dustbin of history when heroic deeds had survived orally despite lack of records. The deeds of the modern day so-called heroes are better ego-fanning acts that are dwarfed by ethnic heroes of the past. National service has become wealth acquisition service whereas the legends in the folklore were indeed true heroes of their time rendering selfless services to their people without the motive for self-aggrandizement, which today is the bane of our leaders. Though the heroes were ethnic heroes may be ethicizing the deeds of our heroes would put them in better shape amongst their people.

Understanding the facts and accepting it as it is that Nigeria was a contraption that had progressed better under the watchful eyes of the British guns and military whips of the colonialists will help us see the need to retrace where we were coming from, determine where we are and decide where we are going. After over forty years of independence, the nation has not progressed despite being so rich. Things have been worse than the colonialists left them bearing in mind that there was no crude oil in Nigeria then. The pretence of our non-existing unity has caused more frictions in the nation polity. This has led to occasional outbreak of violence in several parts of the nation.

True path to the evolution of natural and truly independent nation had been missed through the ambitions of the colonialists. However, Nigeria can no longer continue to bask in the darkness of ignorance while the leaders pretend that all is well. Since 1914, all have not been well. Not just since 1914, all had never ever been well since the British set foot on the Nigerian soil.

The process and dynamics of change had not been followed leading to the formation of one true nation where peace, justice, equal right and respect for the dignity of the black man irrespective of race, tribe, tongue and religion would reign. A society where there would be no second class citizens and opportunities abound for all. In the pre-colonial Nigeria, the empires respected their citizens and held them in high esteem; slaves were mostly tributes and spoils of war. No community would unnecessarily infringe on the right of neighboring community for fear of reprisal.

This is the kind of Nigeria that the average Nigerian desires and God willing he seeks to have, a Nigeria where the future is brightly determined by the actions of today. A Nigeria that those generations yet unborn would be proud of and be indeed proud of her history of evolution while cohabiting in peace and true unity.

CHAPTER TWO

<u>ECONOMIES OF STATES IN PRE-COLONIAL NIGERIA</u>

It is a common thinking in the present Nigeria that the major ethnic groups seem to hold on to the present arrangement of Nigeria for economic reasons. The contraption foisted on the people of Nigeria seems to suit them especially now that they seem to have lost hope of quick economic revival if the arrangement is tampered with. The crude oil trade seems to have provided cheap wealth for the development of their homeland to the detriment of the oil producing areas. Thus any attempt at restructuring is being erroneously resisted by a lazy generation that seems to squander the legacy bequeathed by nature.

The pre-colonial Nigeria had been made up of self-sustaining communities. These communities had evolved an economic system that was immune to the present economic postulation of modern day theorists. The colonialists were themselves beneficiaries of these buoyant economies as it was the same African economy that led Europe out of the lull that her economy was experiencing at the time. These same colonialists foist on Africans today, various theories to further sink the dwindling economies of the African states. The driving motive of the scramble for Africa was economic. It was obvious that the pre-colonial Nigeria and Africa had a better and virgin economy with full potential for growth than the Europeans' home economy had that they began to crave plundering it.

The colonialists had migrated from homeland into various parts of the new-found lands and Africa was the ground for the provision of the labor required for the development of the new-found lands. At home the Europeans were experiencing dwindling economic fortunes, rising unemployment, increased crime rates and unprecedented poverty that a scramble for African wealth soon generate friction among the superpowers. Rather than engage in a world war for the soul of Africa, the Europeans called a conference to jaw-jaw rather than war-war.

The African State had all that was needed for all of them to develop their homelands; after all, she had provided all the manpower needed to develop the new-found lands in the slave trade era. The trade with Africa had produced a series of noveau rich Europeans who bore allegiance only to home crowns as well as powerful and rich African leaders who had become laws to themselves like the Jaja of Opobo, Nana Olomu Itshekiri.

For more than a century, European economy was sustained by the African State. European industries were fed with raw materials from Africa. The case of Britain was interesting as it was plundering all the way in all her colonies. The gluttonous nature of the British and the Dutch were unequalled in history. In all the colonies of these two colonialists, a new dimension was introduced that was color distinct that is apartheid, from which the entire world fought to liberate the soul of humanity that the Europeans had debased. In every colony they made it clear to the subjects that they were liberated animals from the jungle while engaging in unparalleled plundering of the colonies.

As the raw materials from the so-called jungle seemed inexhaustible, the thirst of the colonialists became insatiable. The British, the Portuguese and the Dutch who were the major trade partners of the Niger-Delta area as well as the Niger Area then became ambitious. Certain chiefs and trade middlemen who were becoming too powerful and wise in the ways of the Europeans must be eliminated. This was to enable the Europeans get to the roots of commodity trade and avoid the double standards of their middlemen who were behaving like harlots going to the highest bidder irrespective of trade agreement. Thus leaders like Nana Olomu, Jaja of Opobo etc had to go. Their superior firepower made that possible as the guns soon boomed against all resistance.

Various communities and empires before the advent of the Europeans had lived and traded in the pre-colonial Nigeria and some notable areas have become trade routes and trade towns. At the close of the 19th century, a more cohesive trade relationship had been developed amongst the tribes of the Niger-Delta than it is today. While the Yoruba States were engaged in a civil war, the Itshekiri, Urhobos, Ijaws and the rest of the Niger Delta tribes were thriving in trade with the Europeans towards the coast.

Individually, the old states that today make up the present day Nigeria had developed their own economy that was dictated by their environment and their culture. Their economy was also dependent on their neighbors with whom they had interacted. The Nigeria pre-colonial economy was so much dependent on subsistent production. This made self-sustenance possible, as everyone was a producer. Where production exceeded the need of the individual, it goes into the community and where the need of the community had been satisfied then, a trade with near neighbors is established.

The Nigeria States in pre-colonial times had thrived economically without depending on the neighboring economy. The pre-colonial Hausa States for example had thrived on the production of millet, guinea corn, tomatoes, vegetables etc. There was also a tax system that had been entrenched in the administration of the state that ensured that the political organs ran smoothly. These were the *'jingali'* a tax imposed on cows and goats produced within the system and the *'gandu'* a tax imposed on the conquered territories. These tax systems were in operation before the jihad.

The first attempt at a unified Hausa state was the jihad of Othman Dan Fodio 1804-1809. This established the Sokoto Caliphate with Sokoto becoming the new political and religious centre of the North. The Hausas were also producers of hides and skin. They had become very popular in this trade that their skins were traded as far as the North of Africa to the Berbers in the Sahara desert.

The mainstay of the Hausa economy was similar in the entire Northern Region, farming, animal husbandry and salt production in areas along the Niger-Benue confluence area. The Igalas combined these with pottery making, weaving, beer brewing and handicraft. The Jukuns had also established a strong tax system along side their trade in yam, beniseed and salt. These Northern groups traded to develop a self-sufficient economy, in which they had become self-actualized and by so doing realized their potentials.

In the South, by late fifteenth century, when the first Europeans visited Benin, they met a well-developed political and economic system that saw the kingdom thriving. Of all the kingdoms, Benin kingdom had built a guild system that saw all trade as affiliation of the political system. That is, all the guilds were affiliated to the palace. Each of these guilds had their own quarters and people of similar trade and orientation lived together in their own quarters. Thus you have the carvers, brass workers, blacksmiths, drummers, butchers, iron casters, leather workers, ivory carvers, priests and diviners living in separate communities. By 1504, the Binis had begun to send ambassadors to Portugal as recognized sovereign state.

A century after in 1604, the kingdom could be compared with other European kingdoms, Benin City was compared with great cities like Amsterdam and the streets were described as seven to eight times wider than those in Amsterdam. Even though Benin had begun to decline before the British invasion of 1897, it stood its ground against the British treaties that annexed the African land. The economy of Benin was broadly developed that even the Europeans recognized its sovereignty.

In the other kingdoms of Oyo, agriculture was the mainstay of the economy. Kola nut was a major product of the kingdom as well as cloth making and other carved items. These were traded with other states like the Nupes and the Hausas who had become conversant with their neighbors within the region. The Ibos were great merchant traders of the oil palm as the Ijaws, the Ilajes and the Itshekiris to the Delta were great fishermen and boat makers.

The economic development of the Nigerian State had spanned over three centuries with the states developing independently before the Europeans came. The colonial masters came at the time of major industrial crisis in their home occasioned by inflation and the need for raw material. The labour to cultivate the new-found land was also a driving motive. Their coming initially bore the disguise of blessing for the African states. Their trade in arms soon enriched powerful African states as the urge for territorial conquest increased among the natural rulers.

The ambition to be free also increased as new states and powers began to spring up among the initially weak ones. It became easy for every powerful military man to question the authority of the kings. Thus rich and powerful men began to declare their own kingdoms. Also, states that had become tired of paying tribute began to fight for liberation. All these were due to the gun trade. Moreover, the essence of the gun trade was for the colonialists to get to the root of the raw materials as these guns were mostly sold to the middlemen who use them to raid for slaves and raw materials that were commodities of trade with the whites.

The Europeans gained more from the trade terms as raw materials soon found their ways to the industries in Europe that processed them and transported them back to be sold at exorbitant prices to the same people that had produced the raw materials. This prevented the collapse of the European economy as the colonialists began to redraw the boundaries and kingdoms of Africa for and on behalf of Africans without the participation of Africans.

Thus, the stage was set for the great plunder that was in the making as the history of Africa was being rewritten politically and economically.

The advent of the British into Nigeria killed the resolve of certain portions of the union to develop their potential economically as they began to depend on subsidy and grant-in-aid from the other parts and Britain to survive. This dependence was also to lead to the great mistake known as the amalgamation of the two countries without the consensus opinion of the people so affected so long as it was to serve the economic interest of the colonialists.

Despite the inherent imbalance in the arrangement, the British still went ahead to amalgamate the North and the South of Nigeria. This imbalance was nurtured by the colonialists through the feudalistic tendencies of the Northern elite using the instrument of indirect rule system of government. This greatly served the purpose of the colonialists, as the feudal lords became stooges in the hands of the British through which the people were further attacked and debased. The Northern class consciousness and personality worship became inherent in a region already disoriented and held down by retrogressive force seeking to continue their hold on the already extinct kingdoms that become only phantoms confined to the bin of memories.

The British in the amalgamation of the North and South of Nigeria brought together under one political and economic unit, states that had hitherto run independent political and economic systems of government. In the slave trade era, the Europeans respected this independence as terms of trade were respected. The colonialists initially recognized the sovereign authority of the individual state it traded with.

As the British colonial master took over completely, they began to dictate productions in the agricultural sector based on their own home needs without regard for what the people knew and were used to. The whole methods were changed and Africans must produce only to suit the changing taste of the colonial masters. The colonies became mere extension of their own metropolitan economies. They must produce only to suit the vogue at home. Africa was thus the farm or the raw material production ground for European companies. The African economy became an extension of the European economy.

African destiny became dependent on the growth of the Europeans. It is a trend that has continued till this day. Recession in the world economy, Europe and the Americas always translate to recession in Africa. The power of independent development that the economies of states in Africa had enjoyed was removed with the colonial ambition of the Europeans who also foisted on Africans political systems alien to Africans. The African economy became completely subjected to the European economy. It is even worse in the French colonies where even the air the people breathe seem to be imported from France.

The system of productions became fashioned along the European pattern. New crops that were alien to African soil were introduced as the need in Europe dictated. This trend continued even after independence. While the Asians discarded all form of European lifestyle after independence, Africans held on to the new life style learnt from their masters as obedient students. Even some tribes became colonies and extension of other bigger ones. The Asians began a new wave of evolution by breaking free of all imperialist thoughts. They became truly independent unlike the African.

The Asians developed their own economies by tinkering with the pattern left by the colonialists and breaking loose of imperialism of the neo-colonial era. Their political and economic system evolved without undue recourse to the colonialists' theories and undue interference. Their economies had come out strong after undergoing series of turbulent periods. The people had evolved an enduring economic system.

The power to independently develop regional potential of states in Africa became lost as the stolen opportunities left with the Europeans whose post colonial African states became the weeping children of the world. They started begging for more aids from same people and continent that had depended on her economy for development centuries ago.

CHAPTER THREE

NIGERIA: THE ROAD TO NATIONHOOD

When the Europeans first landed in the Kingdom of Benin in the 1406, little did the people of the kingdom know that the course of their history was about to be rewritten and altered. The kingdom was on the course of being subjected to foreign economy and strange political life under the Nigeria State. The grandeur and the splendor of the state awed the Europeans that they saw so much to be desired. They saw so much waste. So many things that would yield fortunes in Europe that were of little or no use in Africa.

Then their visit to the Itshekiri kingdoms and trade emissaries to these kingdoms, interstate exchange of visit of prominent African leaders like Don Domingo to Europe began to lay the foundation for greedy European take-over of the African territories and the domination of their political and economic lives.

First, it began in the form of harmless trade missions, then the slave trades as African leaders saw more power in the mouth of the gun given as commodity of trade by the Europeans in exchange for the slaves captured from African homelands. After that came the era of commodity trades which saw Europeans greatly exploiting the African in terms of trade. The dangers began to manifest when Europeans began to force protection treaties down the throat of leaders using threats of attack. The weaker regions soon rushed into the treaties believing same to give them liberation from the more powerful states. The wise ones refused knowing full well that they would not need anyone to protect them, rather they were the protectors of their own kingdom.

The European governments began to grant charters to companies on African land and on African soil as if they were part of their dominions. African states began to be run like the extensions of European kingdoms of the times. Exclusive trade rights were granted companies from Europe not by African leaders but by European kings and queens. These were informed by the desire to control the trade routes from Africa by the super power nations then. Thus the British granted the Royal Niger Company the charter to the Niger Area to exclusively trade on behalf of the United Kingdom of Britain. As trade became more competitive and the African middlemen became wiser in the ways of the Europeans, it appeared there was a clash of interest between the Europeans as they began to outdo each other. As their greed became pronounced and the African middlemen began to exploit it knowing how invaluable the raw materials from his soil had become to the white man, he began the highest-bidder-grab-it trade. In their bid to avoid clashing with each other, the white men had to identify the middlemen as their common enemy.

The desire to eliminate the middlemen who like the European had become too wise and greedy in the ways of the European led to the scramble for the African land. Having identified their common enemies, the Europeans called a conference amongst themselves to decide the fate of another people, another tribe, another race, another creation and another land without any representation from the people whose fate were been decided. The super powers, Britain, Germany, France,

Spain and Portugal sat down in the 1884/1885 Berlin conference to partition Africa amongst themselves.

Delimitation of boundaries was their exclusive right. The sovereignty of the states being partitioned was jettisoned and any tribe or nation that finds itself within the portion so ceded to any of the super power nations so must remain to be governed. Another authority became subjected to another authority, another sovereignty discarded because of superior power of the gun. After the partitioning, African Kings became subjects of foreign kings and queens. These European kings and queens did not even know what their subject states looked like save for the reports brought to them by subjects who represented them in these foreign lands. It was this Berlin conference that saw to the birth of modern Nigeria State in 1885. Before then, Lagos had been initially declared a protectorate of the British Government in 1865. The implication of the Berlin conference was that the super powers must do everything possible within their power to bring the independent states of Africa under their subjection. Between 1885 and 1900, the entire African country apart from Ethiopia had come under the European powers through military expeditions.

By 1900, Africans had begun to wake up to the realities of another land another people another race deciding their destiny. The right of the African to evolve had been taken away. The fate of the people had been decided by another race from strange land. For their own economic and political interest, the future of the African child was stolen, his right to determine his future became null. It was decided in Berlin that the African needed liberation from his jungle, the jungle that provided food of the European, the jungle that had saved the European economy from collapse.

Africans were forced to live together against their wish by the Europeans due to their own selfish economic interest. The desire to lump strange bedfellows together by the Europeans was not borne out of concern for the system but for administrative convenience. Nigeria was a result of this motive. All kinds of people who had hitherto run their own state and economy were brought to live together as one state without giving them a say in the decision to have them live together.

The motive to bring the people of Nigeria together by the British after the Berlin conference had no such considerations as cultural unity or political unity as existed in the pre-colonial Nigeria. They began by the systematic conquest of the kingdoms that were within the delimited boundaries assigned to them in Berlin. From Warri, Koko, Benin, Opobo, Oyo, down to Sokoto, Maiduguri, all fell to the guns of the colonialists except areas that opted to willingly sign the protection accord ceding all their territories to the British. Thus was born the contraption Nigeria. Having subdued all oppositions, in January 1914, the British again without due consideration for the will of the people amalgamated the North and Southern Protectorates. These two separate entities had hitherto shared little to nothing in common in terms of cultural and linguistic affinity, to warrant the forming of a single nation. The decision that was unanimously taken by the colonialists was taken for administrative and economic reasons.

The burden of building the Nigeria State in the pattern of the British nation became enormous for the British who soon discovered that the entire Niger Area was not as viable as they had thought. It soon dawned on them that the North was not an economically viable whole. The burden of building modern state to support

44

their quest for economic dominance soon began to face financial difficulties in the North. Thus construction of the basic infrastructure needed to facilitate movement of produce to the port towns became burden that the Northern Region economy could not support.

In order to meet its administrative needs in the North, the colonial authorities began by borrowing money from the South. In the early years, the South contributed to the finances of the North. For the first three years, the South contributed an annual subsidy of £33,000. The British government also provided grant-in-aid to the North, as even the subsidy from the South was not enough to meet its administrative needs. The grant in aid rose from £83,000 in 1900 to £405,000 four years later and by the end of 1910 it had declined to £277,000. With these deficits in the North and the surplus in the South being recorded the British came to the conclusion that amalgamating the two regions was inevitable. This would enable the administration reduce the British grants as surplus from the South would be used for developmental needs of the North.

It was evident that the 1914 amalgamation of the Northern and Southern Protectorates of Nigeria brought together, assorted strange elements without respect for their wish to live together. These strange elements came in the form of Islamic feudal emirates, pagan states, Christianized states, port towns, large markets, and centralized and non-centralized states. Most of these states had history of hostility towards each other which only proper dialogue and the natural process of evolution would have removed. By the amalgamation according to John Hatch (1970) in his 'Nigeria History' certain questions were left unanswered, these were;

- What would be the effect of uniting the Fulani emirates – with their static traditional outlook – with the thrusting, competitive, individualistic society of the South, now acquiring knowledge from growing number of mission schools which were making available an expanding clerical class?
- How would societies that only a few years earlier were rivals and often-hostile states live together under one administration?
- Should they form a single nation?
- If so how could true allegiance to the state be created?
- In any case what was the objective of the British policy?
- Was it to build an empire permanently subordinate to Britain to act as a trustee for some shadowy African future or to encourage a natural spirit leading to ultimate governance?

These questions were left unanswered by the colonialists and even as John Hatch saw it in 1970, these questions are still unanswered in the nation over fifty years of independence. The amalgamation did not unite the two protectorates; it had rather made the differences in the two regions inherent and exposed the plot of the British to continually keep Nigerians in perpetual colonialism.

CHAPTER FOUR

<u>NIGERIA AFTER AMALGAMATION</u>

The post amalgamated Nigeria presents an interesting study. It brought to fore, the flaws in amalgamation and further brought out the selfish interest of the British in the exercise. The British customs became laws and they administered the land according to their laws. They only allowed the local chiefs to participate in justice where it is a matter of tradition. Every other thing was judged according to British standard. The South was governed differently from the North. Different measures were used which of course has led to further division among the people.

Rather than grow into one unique entity, it had grown into various distinct nations. Government was the exclusive right of the British as only the colonialist passed laws. The late Herbert Macaulay who formed the Nigeria National Democratic Party to contest the 1922 elections for the Lagos Legislative Council led the first attempt at Nigerian participation in governance. The party was limited to the Lagos area.

The first organization that was national in outlook was the Nigeria Youth Movement, which was formed in 1936. It had the likes of Samuel Akinsanya, H. O. Davis, Ernest Ikoli and Dr. J. C. Vaughan as leaders. Chief Obafemi Awolowo and Dr. Nnamdi Azikiwe were also members. Despite its national outlook, the NYM was still a Southern affair without Northern participation. NYM did not exist for up to ten years before internal crisis saw that it became moribund in 1941.

The break up of the NYM led to the formation of a more nationalist party in the NCNC (the National Council of Nigeria and Cameroon) on August 26th 1944. Herbert Macaulay was its president while Dr Nnamdi Azikiwe was its national secretary.

The party was an umbrella union for trade unions, small and local parties, tribal unions and literary groups. However, national distrust soon set into the party as the Ibo elements in the party began to gradually hijack the party machinery. In a bid to protect their tribal interests, other tribes especially the major tribes began to pull out to form their own tribal parties that cater for the interest of their tribal enclave.

This led to the formation of the Action Group by Chief Obafemi Awolowo, using his Egbe Om'Oduduwa Cultural group as a launching pad in 1948. It had its base entrenched in the Yoruba hinterland. The North came up with the Northern Peoples Congress in 1949 led by Sir Ahmadu Bello, the Sardauna of Sokoto and Abubakar Tafawa Balewa. This party was also an offshoot of Jamiyar Mutanen Arewa formerly led by Dr. R. A. Dikko, the first medical doctor from the North. The NPC due to ideological differences soon split into two. Mallam Aminu Kano went to form the Northern Element Progressive Union, incorporating the less privileged as NPC remained the party for the elite.

The emerging scenarios above began to set the stage for tribal politics in Nigeria. It also set the stage for the domination of the landscape by the so-called tribal tripods of Nigeria. The forefathers of tribal politics in Nigeria were setting the stage for further disunity. The road to independent statehood was thus laced with the problems of allegiance to ethnic nationalities rather than for the entity called Nigeria. From then, party activities became regional rather than national. Interests became tribal rather than national. The major tribes had become like hawks waiting to prey on the soul of the nation way before independence. The minorities were thus relegated to the background only as adding up the number to give the parties control.

Right from the beginning of party formations along tribal lines, the stage was getting set for a civil war after independence. The agitators for independence began to withdraw to their regions to become regional champions of tribal course as regional autonomies were granted the regions. This saw Chief Obafemi Awolowo become premier in the West, Dr. Nnamdi Azikiwe in the East and Sir Ahmadu Bello in the North. The East and the West had been granted self-rule two years earlier than the North in 1959.

The first sign of the mistake of amalgamation came to the fore in 1953 when Chief Anthony Enahoro moved the motion for independence by 1956. This was violently resisted in the North to show the disparity in the two regions. Mobs in the Northern City of Kano began to attack Southerners. They burnt and looted houses and mutilated the bodies of their guests. While parties were formed basically to protect the interest of the major ethnic groups, the minorities were left unprotected from the danger of the emerging scenario.

It would seem that only the British propelled the North's desire to remain in the union probably by presenting the realities of the backwardness of the North without the South to its leaders. Sir Ahmadu Bello would later threaten the Governor-general with Northern cessation if the AG and NCNC were allowed to form the central government against the promise of the colonialists to the North to ensure Northern domination of the national polity. The colonialists have been biased umpires in the game to nation building and attainment of independent.

One question that was however left unanswered before and after independent has been the fears of the minorities becoming irrelevant in the politics of the emerging Nigeria nation. The British despite the setting up of commissions of enquiry did not see the need to adequately address the issue before independence. This was in tandem with their resolve to force the people to live together irrespective of their cultural and ethnic differences. This problem has been so peculiar to the area known as the Niger-Delta region. As it would seem, the Northern minorities had integrated perfectly into the idea of a monolithic North as muted by the feudal lords using the machinery of religion and language.

This idea was partially successful for the reason of the earlier jihad and the fact that the entire North had mixed well with the Hausa elements within their societies and had picked Hausa as a second language. Although few leaders like the late Joseph Tarka sought to distinguish themselves from feudal holds. Sokoto was more the political capital of the North than Kaduna as allegiance to Sokoto was stronger than even allegiance to the nation. The Northern minorities saw themselves as being compelled to think and act the script of their Hausa/Fulani overlords who had conquered much of their territories during the jihad.

50

The major tribes namely the Hausas, Yorubas, and the Ibos began to develop the Nigeria of their own dream where each one of them would be the overlord of all. They began to build their regions in accordance with their perceived dreams and desires disregarding the existence of the other tribes. The North seems to have more regard for its minority than did the Yorubas and the Ibos in the early days. Kaduna, the capital city was on minority soil and was seen as home for all unlike Enugu and Ibadan that carried the emblem of tribal politics. When Benin came later as regional headquarter, the minorities identified with it more than did all other capital cities in the south.

The North on the whole had begun to develop a monolithic relationship with its minority. They saw themselves as part of one whole. This was one lesson that the rest of the country would have learnt from the North. They at least saw themselves as one and even the Southerner sees the North as one indistinguishable whole. The cohesion of Sir Ahmadu Bello ensured that this was actually cemented through elitist allegiance to the caliphate. The North distributed every position among Northerners irrespective of language and tongue. The guarding principle was the protection of Northern interest.

As Ahmadu Bello remained in Kaduna to be Premier of the Northern Region, Tafawa Balewa was sent to go to Lagos and become the Prime Minister. At this time, the North had begun to position itself for leadership in the country by fostering unity on its people. Irrespective of tribe and religion, in so much as the Sardauna would have wanted to Islamize the entire country, the elite saw themselves as one, owing allegiance to the Sardauna. They saw the South as one common enemy that must be subdued no matter what. These were basically the thinking of the elite.

Seeing the South has natural assumed economic leadership, the North begun to plan for the future in which it would play political domineering role. This was the vision of the Sardauna who began to encourage the youths to enlist in the army, knowing full well that the South had overtaken it in the pursuit of Western education especially the West. The domineering role of the caliphate and the dynamic political leadership of the Sardauna ensured that the Northern dream was kept alive. The other leaders had come had come to the quick conclusion that they were more advantageously placed to run the nation.

Awolowo and Azikiwe were rather busy trying to scheme out each other than unites for a common course. The two leaders it would seem had so much distrust for each other. While they were engaged in a needless war of supremacy, the Sardauna was busy preparing the Northerners for leadership by building a new military elitist class for the North. The result of the amalgamation of the country had become so glaring that it was obvious that the nation going into independence was not one united and indivisible nation. That the country had survived this far is a miracle. That the country had not split all these while must have been by the hand of some divine powers. When various strange elements are lumped together in one mass without their consenting opinion, the result had never been too good. This is the result from other countries.

The lumping of all ethnic nationalities together as one political entity by the action of the military conquest did more damage than good especially to the psyche of the average minority nationals. The nation has never truly experienced unity; the ethnic nationals had reluctantly been made part of the union whose future they did not envisage. Thus Benin kingdom reluctantly after a bloody war became part of the union, Oyo kingdom did not opt to become part of the union willingly, Nana of Itshekiri had to be subdued to annex his territories, King Jaja of Opobo was banished and so were other ethnic nationals.

No ethnic nationality consented to the dubious treaties of the colonialists who forcefully brought them under one umbrella union and made a single economy and single political unit, states, which only few years back had absolute control of their economy and political machinery. To achieve the measure of unity that the North had attained, religion became the opium. The caliphate had to stamp its authority on the emirates. Another plus was that the minorities had quickly picked Hausa as a second language as these were the major palace language and of the jihad scholars and teachers.

As the North was preparing to take hold of the nation's political life from the colonialists, Chief Obafemi Awolowo was preparing the Yorubas for economic empowerment and enlightenment through his welfarist programmes. He created the free education that ensured that the Yorubas acquired minimal education that would liberate them from the shackles of poverty and hold by unfavorable tendencies. The East it would seem had no clear ideological path even to unite the Ibos as one let alone the minorities among them. The activities of the Catholic Church amongst them were what attempted to place them in the light of educational attainment.

Dr. Nnamdi Azikiwe is today best remembered as one of the founding fathers of the nation, and first ceremonial president of Nigeria for his oratorical prowess than for any ideology or popular programmes as the other two regional leaders. Though he steadfastly believed in one true Nigeria where everyone is equal, he equally believed in it in just the way that it was handed over to them by the colonialists. The only person that had no such faith in Nigeria was Sir Ahmadu Bello. He saw the disparity in the nation but erroneously believed that it was the North that was at disadvantage. He thus, went on to implement a Northern agenda that soon saw the North as the dominating force of the union.

The minorities were to take their destiny in their hands, having no one to truly fight their course as it was always the majority having their way and the minority having their say. The first attempt at addressing the minority agitation was the Willink Commission of 1958 shortly before the colonialists left. The commission went out to examine the basis of the fear of the minority in independent Nigeria and made recommendations.

The recommendations were more of advice to the political class than recommendations for implementation. The choice of allaying the fears of the minorities was left in the hands of the political class. The (political class) were more interested in their positions as political leaders, than building a virile nation and changing the general orientations of Nigerians as distinct people, to that of a people with common destiny within a true federal union.

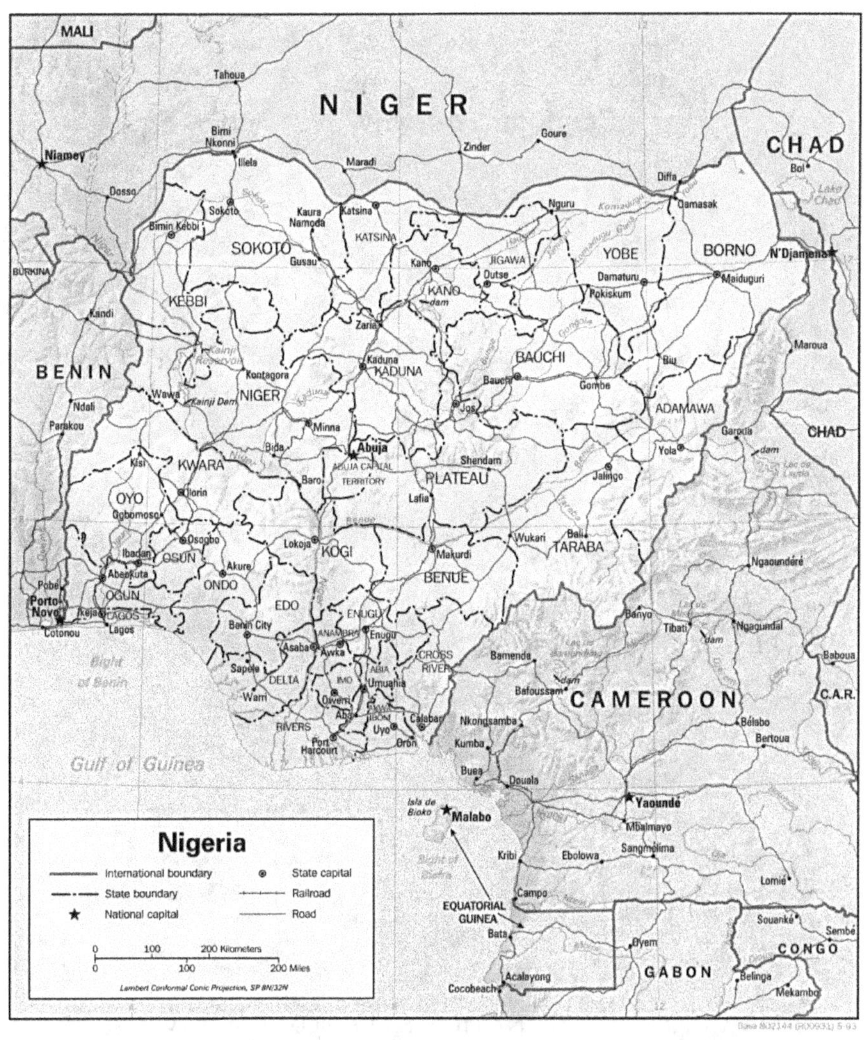

MAP OF NIGERIA SHOWING THE 36 STATES OF NIGERIA

Economic Activity

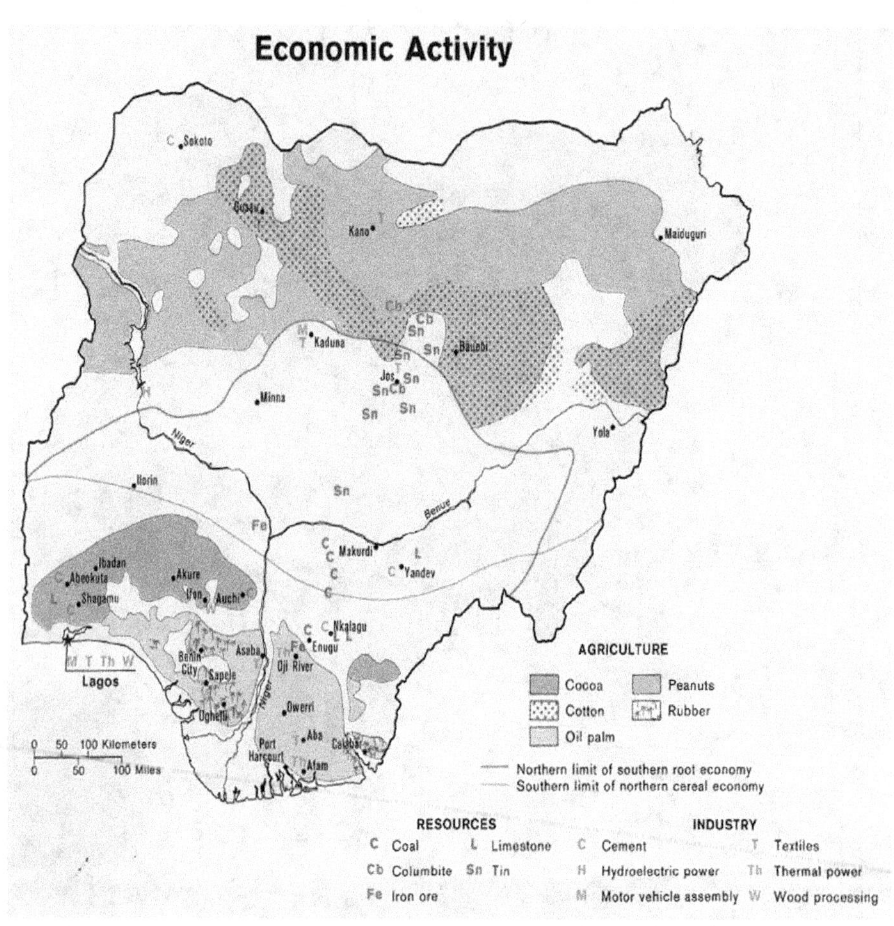

MAP SHOWING THE NATION'S ECONOMIC ACTIVITIES

<u>*NIGERIA FACT FILE*</u>

<u>Background:</u>

British influence and control over what would become Nigeria and Africa's most populous country grew through the 19th century. A series of constitutions after World War II granted Nigeria greater autonomy; independence came in 1960. Following nearly 16 years of military rule, a new constitution was adopted in 1999, and a peaceful transition to civilian government was completed. The government continues to face the daunting task of reforming a petroleum-based economy, whose revenues have been squandered through corruption and mismanagement, and institutionalizing democracy. In addition, Nigeria continues to experience longstanding ethnic and religious tensions. Although both the 2003 and 2007 presidential elections were marred by significant irregularities and violence, Nigeria is currently experiencing its longest period of civilian rule since independence. The general elections of April 2007 marked the first civilian-to-civilian transfer of power in the country's history and the elections of 2011 were generally regarded as credible. In January 2014, Nigeria assumed a nonpermanent seat on the UN Security Council for the 2014-15 term.

<u>*Geography*</u>

Location: *Western Africa, bordering the Gulf of Guinea, between Benin and Cameroon*
Geographic coordinates: *10 00 N, 8 00 E*
Map references: *Africa*
Total Area: *923,768 sq km*
country comparison to the world: 32
land: 910,768 sq km
water: 13,000 sq km
Area - comparative:slightly more than twice the size of California
Land boundaries:
total: 4,047 km
border countries: Benin 773 km, Cameroon 1,690 km, Chad 87 km, Niger 1,497 km
Coastline: 853 km
Maritime claims: territorial sea: 12 nm
exclusive economic zone: 200 nm
continental shelf: 200 m depth or to the depth of exploitation

Climate: varies; equatorial in south, tropical in center, arid in north

Terrain: southern lowlands merge into central hills and plateaus; mountains in southeast, plains in northElevation extremes:
lowest point: Atlantic Ocean 0 m
highest point: Chappal Waddi 2,419 m

Natural resources:

natural gas, petroleum, tin, iron ore, coal, limestone, niobium, lead, zinc, arable land
Land use: *arable land: 38.97%, permanent crops: 3.46%, other: 57.57% (2011)*
Irrigated land: *2,932 sq km (2004)*
Total renewable water resources: 286.2 cu km (2011)
Freshwater withdrawal (domestic/industrial/agricultural):
total: 13.11 cu km/yr (31%/15%/54%)
Per capita: *89.21 cu m/yr (2005)*
Natural hazards:periodic droughts; flooding
Environment - current issues: soil degradation; rapid deforestation; urban air and water pollution; desertification; oil pollution - water, air, and soil; has suffered serious damage from oil spills; loss of arable land; rapid urbanization
Environment - international agreements:
Party to: *Biodiversity, Climate Change, Climate Change-Kyoto Protocol, Desertification, Endangered Species, Hazardous Wastes, Law of the Sea, Marine Dumping, Marine Life Conservation, Ozone Layer Protection, Ship Pollution, Wetlands*
signed, but not ratified: none of the selected agreements
Geography - note: *the Niger enters the country in the northwest and flows southward through tropical rain forests and swamps to its delta in the Gulf of Guinea*
People and Society : Nigeria
Nationality:
noun: Nigerian(s)
adjective: Nigerian
Ethnic groups:
Nigeria, Africa's most populous country, is composed of more than 250 ethnic groups; the following are the most populous and politically influential: Hausa and Fulani 29%, Yoruba 21%, Igbo (Ibo) 18%, Ijaw 10%, Kanuri 4%, Ibibio 3.5%, Tiv 2.5%
Languages:
English (official), Hausa, Yoruba, Igbo (Ibo), Fulani, over 500 additional indigenous languages

58

Religions: *Muslim 50%, Christian 40%, indigenous beliefs10%*
Population: *177,155,754 (July 2014 est.)*
country comparison to the world: 8
note: estimates for this country explicitly take into account the effects of excess mortality due to AIDS; this can result in lower life expectancy, higher infant mortality, higher death rates, lower population growth rates, and changes in the distribution of population by age and sex than would otherwise be expected
Age structure:
0-14 years: 43.2% (male 39,151,304/female 37,353,737)
15-24 years: 19.3% (male 17,486,117/female 16,732,533)
25-54 years: 30.5% (male 27,697,644/female 26,285,816)
55-64 years: 3.1% (male 3,393,631/female 3,571,301)
65 years and over: 3% (male 2,621,845/female 2,861,826) (2014 est.)
Dependency ratios:
total dependency ratio: 89 %
youth dependency ratio: 83.8 %
elderly dependency ratio: 5.2 %
potential support ratio: 19.3 (2013)
Median age:total: 18.2 years
male: 18.1 years
female: 18.3 years (2014 est.)
Population growth rate: *2.47% (2014 est.)*
country comparison to the world: 33
Birth rate: *38.03 births/1,000 population (2014 est.)*
country comparison to the world: 12
Death rate: *13.16 deaths/1,000 population (2014 est.)*
country comparison to the world: 19
Net migration rate: *-0.22 migrant(s)/1,000 population (2014 est.)*
country comparison to the world: 120
Urbanization:
urban population: 49.6% of total population (2011)
rate of urbanization: 3.75% annual rate of change (2010-15 est.)
Major urban areas - population:
Lagos 10.203 million; Kano 3.304 million; Ibadan 2.762 million; ABUJA (capital) 1.857 million; Kaduna 1.519 million (2009)
Sex ratio:
at birth: 1.06 male(s)/female
0-14 years: 1.05 male(s)/female
15-24 years: 1.05 male(s)/female
25-54 years: 1.05 male(s)/female

55-64 years: 1.04 male(s)/female
65 years and over: 0.85 male(s)/female
total population: 1.01 male(s)/female (2014 est.)
Mother's mean age at first birth: 20.9 (2008 est.)
Maternal mortality rate: 630 deaths/100,000 live births (2010)
country comparison to the world: 11
Infant mortality rate: *74.09 deaths/1,000 live births*
country comparison to the world: 10
male: 79.02 deaths/1,000 live births
female: 68.87 deaths/1,000 live births (2014 est.)
Life expectancy at birth:
total population: 52.62 years
country comparison to the world: 212
male: 51.63 years
female: 53.66 years (2014 est.)
Total fertility rate:*5.25 children born/woman (2014 est.)*
country comparison to the world: 13
Contraceptive prevalence rate:14.1% (2011)
Health expenditures: 5.3% of GDP (2011)
country comparison to the world: 127
Physicians density:
0.4 physicians/1,000 population (2008)
Hospital bed density: 0.53 beds/1,000 population (2004)
Drinking water source:
improved:
urban: 75.1% of population
rural: 47.3% of population
total: 61.1% of population
unimproved:
urban: 24.9% of population
rural: 52.7% of population
total: 38.9% of population (2011 est.)
Sanitation facility access:
improved:
urban: 33.2% of population
rural: 28.1% of population
total: 30.6% of population
unimproved:
urban: 66.8% of population
rural: 71.9% of population
total: 69.4% of population (2011 est.)

HIV/AIDS - adult prevalence rate:
3.1% (2012 est.)
country comparison to the world: 20
HIV/AIDS - people living with HIV/AIDS:
3,426,600 (2012 est.)
country comparison to the world: 2
HIV/AIDS - deaths:
239,700 (2012 est.)
country comparison to the world: 1
Major infectious diseases:
degree of risk: very high
food or waterborne diseases: bacterial and protozoal diarrhea, hepatitis A and E, and typhoid fever
vectorborne diseases: malaria, dengue fever, and yellow fever
water contact diseases: leptospirosis and schistosomiasis
respiratory disease: meningococcal meningitis
aerosolized dust or soil contact disease: one of the most highly endemic areas for Lassa fever
animal contact disease: rabies
note: highly pathogenic H5N1 avian influenza has been identified in this country; it poses a negligible risk with extremely rare cases possible among US citizens who have close contact with birds (2013)
Obesity - adult prevalence rate: 6.5% (2008)
country comparison to the world: 146
Children under the age of 5 years underweight: 24.4% (2011)
country comparison to the world: 26
Education expenditures: NA

Literacy:
definition: age 15 and over can read and write
total population: 61.3%
male: 72.1%
female: 50.4% (2010 est.)
School life expectancy (primary to tertiary education):
total: 9 years
male: 10 years
female: 8 years (2005)
Child labor - children ages 5-14:
total number: 11,396,823
percentage: 29 % (2007 est.)

Government
Country name: conventional long form: Federal Republic of Nigeria

conventional short form: Nigeria
Government type: federal republic
Capital: Abuja
geographic coordinates: 9 05 N, 7 32 E
time difference: UTC+1 (6 hours ahead of Washington, DC during Standard Time)
Administrative divisions:
36 states and 1 territory; Abia, Adamawa, Akwa Ibom, Anambra, Bauchi, Bayelsa, Benue, Borno, Cross River, Delta,*
Ebonyi, Edo, Ekiti, Enugu, Federal Capital Territory, Gombe, Imo, Jigawa, Kaduna, Kano, Katsina, Kebbi, Kogi, Kwara,*
Lagos, Nasarawa, Niger, Ogun, Ondo, Osun, Oyo, Plateau, Rivers, Sokoto, Taraba, Yobe, Zamfara
Independence: 1 October 1960 (from the UK)
National holiday: Independence Day (National Day), 1 October (1960)
Constitution: several previous; latest adopted 5 May 1999, effective 29 May 1999; amended 2010
Legal system:
mixed legal system of English common law, Islamic law (in 12 northern states), and traditional law
International law organization participation: accepts compulsory ICJ jurisdiction with reservations; accepts ICCt jurisdiction
Suffrage: 18 years of age; universal
Executive branch:
chief of state: President Mohammadu Buhari (since 29 May 2015);

note - the president is both the chief of state and head of government; Buhari assumed the presidency on 29th May 2015 following the victory of his party over the incumbent President Goodluck JONATHAN who was elected president on 16 April 201.
elections: president elected by popular vote for a four-year term (eligible for a second term)

Legislative branch:
bicameral National Assembly consists of the Senate (109 seats, 3 from each state plus 1 from Abuja; members elected
by popular vote to serve four-year terms) and House of Representatives (360 seats; members elected by popular vote to serve four-year terms)

Judicial branch:

highest court(s): Supreme Court (consists of the chief justice and 15 justices) judge selection and term of office: judges appointed by the president on the recommendation of the National Judicial Council, a 23-member independent body of federal and state judicial officials; judge appointments confirmed by the Senate; judges serve until age 65 subordinate courts: Court of Appeal; Federal High Court; High Court of the Federal Capital Territory; Sharia Court of Appeal of the Federal Capital Territory; Customary Court of Appeal of the Federal Capital Territory; state court system similar in structure to federal system

Political pressure groups and leaders:

Academic Staff Union for Universities or ASUU
Campaign for Democracy or CD
Civil Liberties Organization or CLO
Committee for the Defense of Human Rights or CDHR
Constitutional Right Project or CRP
Human Right Africa
National Association of Democratic Lawyers or NADL
National Association of Nigerian Students or NANS
Nigerian Bar Association or NBA
Nigerian Labor Congress or NLC
Nigerian Medical Association or NMA
the press
Universal Defenders of Democracy or UDD

International organization participation:

ACP, AfDB, AU, C, CD, D-8, ECOWAS, EITI (compliant country), FAO, G-15, G-24, G-77, IAEA, IBRD, ICAO, ICC (national committees), ICRM, IDA, IDB, IFAD, IFC, IFRCS, IHO, ILO, IMF, IMO, IMSO, Interpol, IOC, IOM, IPU, ISO, ITSO, ITU, ITUC (NGOs), MIGA, MINURSO, MINUSMA, MONUSCO, NAM, OAS (observer), OIC, OPCW, OPEC, PCA, UN, UN Security Council (temporary), UNAMID, UNCTAD, UNESCO, UNHCR, UNIDO, UNIFIL, UNISFA, UNITAR, UNMIL, UNMISS, UNOCI, UNWTO, UPU, WCO, WFTU (NGOs), WHO, WIPO, WMO, WTO

Diplomatic representation in the US:
chancery: 3519 International Court NW, Washington, DC 20008
telephone: [1] (202) 986-8400
FAX: [1] (202) 362-6541
consulate(s) general: Atlanta, New York

Diplomatic representation from the US:
embassy: Plot 1075 Diplomatic Drive, Central District Area, Abuja
mailing address: P. O. Box 5760, Garki, Abuja
telephone: [234] (9) 461-4000
FAX: [234] (9) 461-4171
Flag description:
three equal vertical bands of green (hoist side), white, and green; the color green represents the forests and abundant natural wealth of the country, white stands for peace and unity
National symbol(s):
eagle
National anthem:
name: "Arise Oh Compatriots, Nigeria's Call Obey"
lyrics/music: John A. ILECHUKWU, Eme Etim AKPAN, B. A. OGUNNAIKE, Sotu OMOIGUI and P. O. ADERIBIGBE/Benedict Elide ODIASE
note: adopted 1978; the lyrics are a mixture of five of the top entries in a national contest

Recent Economy

Economy - overview: Following an April 2014 statistical "rebasing" exercise, Nigeria emerged as Africa's largest economy, with 2013 GDP estimated at US$ 502 billion. Oil has been a dominant source of government revenues since the 1970s. Regulatory constraints and security risks have limited new investment in oil and natural gas, and Nigeria's oil production contracted in 2012 and 2013. Nevertheless, the Nigerian economy has continued to grow at a rapid 6-8% per annum (pre-rebasing), driven by growth in agriculture, telecommunications, and services, and the medium-term outlook for Nigeria is good, assuming oil output stabilizes and oil prices remain strong. Fiscal authorities pursued countercyclical policies in 2011-2013, significantly reducing the budget deficit. Monetary policy has also been responsive and effective. Following the 2008-9 global financial crises, the banking sector was effectively recapitalized and regulation enhanced. Despite its strong fundamentals, oil-rich Nigeria has been hobbled by inadequate power supply, lack of infrastructure, delays in the passage of legislative reforms, an inefficient property registration system, restrictive trade policies, an inconsistent regulatory environment, a slow and ineffective judicial system, unreliable dispute resolution mechanisms,insecurity, and pervasive corruption. Economic diversification and strong growth have not translated into a significant decline in poverty levels - over

62% of Nigeria's 170 million people live in extreme poverty. President JONATHAN has established an economic team that includes experienced and reputable members and has announced plans to increase transparency, continue to diversify production, and further improve fiscal management. The government is working to develop stronger public-private partnerships for roads, agriculture, and power.

GDP (purchasing power parity): $478.5 billion (2013 est.)
country comparison to the world: 31
$450.4 billion (2012 est.)
$422.6 billion (2011 est.)
note: data are in 2013 US dollars
GDP (official exchange rate): $292 billion (2013 est.)
GDP - real growth rate: 6.2% (2013 est.)
country comparison to the world: 35
6.6% (2012 est.)
7.4% (2011 est.)
GDP - per capita (PPP): $2,800 (2013 est.)
country comparison to the world: 180
$2,700 (2012 est.)
$2,600 (2011 est.)
note: data are in 2013 US dollars
Gross national saving: 15.5% of GDP (2013 est.)
country comparison to the world: 108
15.9% of GDP (2012 est.)
15.4% of GDP (2011 est.)
GDP - composition, by end use:
household consumption: 50.3%
government consumption: 12.8%
investment in fixed capital: 9.8%
investment in inventories: 0%
exports of goods and services: 49.9%
imports of goods and services: -22.8% (2013 est.)
GDP - composition, by sector of origin:
agriculture: 30.9%
industry: 43%
services: 26% (2012 est.)
Agriculture - products:
cocoa, peanuts, cotton, palm oil, corn, rice, sorghum, millet, cassava (tapioca), yams, rubber; cattle, sheep, goats, pigs; timber; fish

Industries:
crude oil, coal, tin, columbite; rubber products, wood; hides and skins, textiles, cement and other construction
materials, food products, footwear, chemicals, fertilizer, printing, ceramics, steel
Industrial production growth rate: 0.9% (2013 est.)
country comparison to the world: 155
Labor force:51.53 million (2011 est.)
country comparison to the world: 12
Labor force - by occupation:
agriculture: 70%
industry: 10%
services: 20% (1999 est.)
Unemployment rate:
23.9% (2011 est.)
country comparison to the world: 172
4.9% (2011 est.)
Population below poverty line:
70% (2010 est.)
Household income or consumption by percentage share:
lowest 10%: 1.8%
highest 10%: 38.2% (2010 est.)
Distribution of family income - Gini index:
43.7 (2003)
country comparison to the world: 47
50.6 (1997)
Budget:
revenues: $23.85 billion
expenditures: $31.51 billion (2013 est.)
Taxes and other revenues: 8.2% of GDP (2013 est.)
country comparison to the world: 211
Budget surplus (+) or deficit (-): -2.6% of GDP (2013 est.)
country comparison to the world: 109
Public debt: 19.3% of GDP (2013 est.)
country comparison to the world: 135
17.9% of GDP (2012 est.)
Fiscal year: calendar year
Inflation rate (consumer prices): 8.7% (2013 est.)
country comparison to the world: 200
12.2% (2012 est.)
Central bank discount rate: 4.25% (31 December 2010 est.)

country comparison to the world: 59
6% (31 December 2009 est.)
Commercial bank prime lending rate: 15.5% (31 December 2013 est.)
country comparison to the world: 33
16.79% (31 December 2012 est.)
Stock of narrow money: $46.48 billion (31 December 2013 est.)
country comparison to the world: 49
$44.41 billion (31 December 2012 est.)
Stock of broad money: $98.75 billion (31 December 2013 est.)
country comparison to the world: 53
$96.34 billion (31 December 2012 est.)
Stock of domestic credit: $93.46 billion (31 December 2013 est.)
country comparison to the world: 53
$93.5 billion (31 December 2012 est.) Market value of publicly traded shares: $56.39 billion (31 December 2012 est.)
country comparison to the world: 54
$39.27 billion (31 December 2011)
$50.88 billion (31 December 2010 est.)
Current account balance: $16.16 billion (2013 est.)
country comparison to the world: 19
$20.35 billion (2012 est.)
Exports: $93.55 billion (2013 est.)
country comparison to the world: 38
$95.68 billion (2012 est.)

Exports - commodities:
petroleum and petroleum products 95%, cocoa, rubber
Exports - partners: US 16.8%, India 11.5%, Netherlands 8.6%, Spain 7.8%, Brazil 7.6%, UK 5.1%, Germany 4.9%, Japan 4.1%, France 4.1% (2012)
Imports: $55.98 billion (2013 est.)
country comparison to the world: 52
$53.36 billion (2012 est.)

Imports - commodities:
machinery, chemicals, transport equipment, manufactured goods, food and live animals
Imports - partners: China 18.3%, US 10.1%, India 5.5% (2012)
Reserves of foreign exchange and gold: $47.7 billion (31 December 2013 est.)
country comparison to the world: 43
$46.41 billion (31 December 2012 est.)

Debt - external: $15.73 billion (31 December 2013 est.)
country comparison to the world: 86
$13.4 billion (31 December 2012 est.)
Stock of direct foreign investment - at home: $84.56 billion (31 December 2013 est.)
country comparison to the world: 45
$76.75 billion (31 December 2012 est.)
Stock of direct foreign investment - abroad: $9.212 billion (31 December 2013 est.)
country comparison to the world: 56
$7.444 billion (31 December 2012 est.)
Exchange rates: nairas (NGN) per US dollar -
156.8 (2013 est.)
156.81 (2012 est.)
150.3 (2010 est.)
148.9 (2009)
117.8 (2008)

Energy :

Electricity - production: 24.87 billion kWh (2010 est.)
country comparison to the world: 6 8
Electricity - consumption: 20.38 billion kWh (2010 est.)
country comparison to the world: 69
Electricity - exports:0 kWh (2012 est.)
country comparison to the world: 177
Electricity - imports: 0 kWh (2012 est.)
country comparison to the world: 178
Electricity - installed generating capacity: 5.9 million kW (2010 est.)
country comparison to the world: 72
Electricity - from fossil fuels: 67.1% of total installed capacity (2010 est.)
country comparison to the world: 114
Electricity - from nuclear fuels: 0% of total installed capacity (2010 est.)
country comparison to the world: 151
Electricity - from hydroelectric plants: 32.8% of total installed capacity (2010 est.)
country comparison to the world: 70
Electricity - from other renewable sources: 0% of total installed capacity (2010 est.)
country comparison to the world: 209
Crude oil - production: 2.524 million bbl/day (2012 est.)

country comparison to the world: 12
Crude oil - exports: 2.341 million bbl/day (2010 est.)
country comparison to the world: 5
Crude oil - imports: 0 bbl/day (2010 est.)
country comparison to the world: 104
Crude oil - proved reserves: 37.2 billion bbl (1 January 2013 es)
country comparison to the world: 10
Refined petroleum products - production: 101,300 bbl/day (2010 est.)
country comparison to the world: 73
Refined petroleum products - consumption: 271,600 bbl/day (2011 est.)
country comparison to the world: 46
Refined petroleum products - exports: 18,750 bbl/day (2010 est.)
country comparison to the world: 73
Refined petroleum products - imports: 151,700 bbl/day (2010 est.)
country comparison to the world: 38
Natural gas - production: 31.36 billion cu m (2011 est.)
country comparison to the world: 29
Natural gas - consumption: 5.03 billion cu m (2010 est.)
country comparison to the world: 62
Natural gas - exports: 25.96 billion cu m (2011 est.)
country comparison to the world: 16
Natural gas - imports:0 cu m (2011 est.)
country comparison to the world: 106
Natural gas - proved reserves: 5.153 trillion cu m (1 January 2013 es)
country comparison to the world: 9
Carbon dioxide emissions from consumption of energy: 75.96 million Mt (2011 est.)
country comparison to the world: 47

Communications
Telephones - main lines in use: 418,200 (2012)
country comparison to the world: 102
Telephones - mobile cellular: 112.78 million (2012)
country comparison to the world: 10
Telephone system: general assessment: further expansion and modernization of the fixed-line telephone network is needed; network quality remains a problem

domestic: the addition of a second fixed-line provider in 2002 resulted in faster growth but subscribership remains only about 1 per 100 persons; mobile-cellular services growing rapidly, in part responding to the shortcomings of the fixed-line network; multiple cellular providers operate nationally with subscribership base approaching 60 per 100 persons international: country code - 234; landing point for the SAT-3/WASC fiber-optic submarine cable that provides connectivity to Europe and Asia; satellite earth stations - 3 Intelsat (2 Atlantic Ocean and 1 Indian Ocean) (2010)

Broadcast media:

nearly 70 federal government-controlled national and regional TV stations; all 36 states operate TV stations; several private TV stations operational; cable and satellite TV subscription services are available; network of federal government-controlled national, regional, and state radio stations; roughly 40 state government-owned radio stations typically carry their own programs except for news broadcasts; about 20 private radio stations; transmissions of international broadcasters are available (2007)

Internet country code: .ng

Internet hosts: 1,234 (2012)

country comparison to the world: 169

Internet users: 43.989 million (2009)

country comparison to the world: 9

Transportation

Airports: 54 (2013)

country comparison to the world: 8 7

Airports - with paved runways:

total: 4 0

over 3,047 m: 10

2,438 to 3,047 m: 12

1,524 to 2,437 m: 9

914 to 1,523 m: 6

under 914 m: 3 (2013)

Airports - with unpaved runways:

total: 1 4

1,524 to 2,437 m: 2

914 to 1,523 m: 9

under 914 m:

3 (2013)

Heliports:

5 (2013)

Pipelines:condensate 124 km; gas 4,045 km; liquid petroleum gas 164 km; oil 4,441 km; refined products 3,940 km (2013)
Railways:
total: 3,505 km
country comparison to the world: 50
narrow gauge: 3,505 km 1.067-m gauge (2008)
Roadways:
total: 193,200 km
country comparison to the world: 27
paved: 28,980 km
unpaved: 164,220 km (2004)
Waterways:
8,600 km (Niger and Benue rivers and smaller rivers and creeks) (2011)
country comparison to the world: 15
Merchant marine:
total: 8 9
country comparison to the world: 54
by type: cargo 2, chemical tanker 28, liquefied gas 1, passenger/cargo 1, petroleum tanker 56, specialized tanker 1
foreign-owned: 3 (India 1, UK 2)
registered in other countries: 33 (Bahamas 2, Bermuda 11, Comoros 1, Italy 1, Liberia 4, North Korea 1, Panama 6,
Seychelles 1, unknown 6) (2010)
Ports and terminals:
major seaport(s): Bonny Inshore Terminal, Calabar, Lagos
Transportation - note:
the International Maritime Bureau reports the territorial and offshore waters in the Niger Delta and Gulf of Guinea as high risk for piracy and armed robbery against ships; in 2012, 27 commercial vessels were boarded or attacked compared with 10 attacks in 2011; crews were robbed and stores or cargoes stolen; Nigerian pirates have extended the range of their attacks to as far away as Cote d'Ivoire

Military

Military branches:
Nigerian Armed Forces: Army, Navy, Air Force (2013)
Military service age and obligation: 18 years of age for voluntary military service; no conscription (2012)
Manpower available for military service: males age 16-49: 37,087,711

females age 16-49: 35,232,127 (2010 est.)
Manpower fit for military service:
males age 16-49: 20,839,976
females age 16-49: 19,867,683 (2010 est.)
Manpower reaching militarily significant age annually:
male: 1,767,428
female: 1,687,719 (2010 est.)
Military expenditures: 0.89% of GDP (2012)
country comparison to the world: 109
0.98% of GDP (2011)
0.89% of GDP (2010)

Transnational Issues

Disputes - international:
Joint Border Commission with Cameroon reviewed 2002 ICJ ruling on the entire boundary and bilaterally resolved differences, including June 2006 Greentree Agreement that immediately cedes sovereignty of the Bakassi Peninsula to Cameroon with a phase-out of Nigerian control within two years while resolving patriation issues; the ICJ ruled on an equidistance settlement of Cameroon-Equatorial Guinea-Nigeria maritime boundary in the Gulf of Guinea, but imprecisely defined coordinates in the ICJ decision and a sovereignty dispute between Equatorial Guinea and Cameroon over an island at the mouth of the Ntem River all contribute to the delay in implementation; only Nigeria and Cameroon have heeded the Lake Chad Commission's admonition to ratify the delimitation treaty which also includes the Chad-Niger and Niger-Nigeria boundaries; location of Benin-Niger-Nigeria tripoint is unresolved Refugees and internally displaced persons:
refugees (country of origin): 5,299 (Liberia) (2011)
IDPs: undetermined (communal violence between Christians and Muslims, political violence; flooding; forced evictions; competition for resources; displacement is mostly short-term) (2012)

Illicit drugs:

a transit point for heroin and cocaine intended for European, East Asian, and North American markets; consumer of amphetamines; safe haven for Nigerian narcotraffickers operating worldwide; major money-laundering center; massive corruption and criminal activity; Nigeria has improved some anti-money-laundering controls, resulting in its removal from the Financial Action Task Force's (FATF's) Noncooperative Countries and Territories List in June

2006; Nigeria's anti-money-laundering regime continues to be monitored by FATF

SOURCE: CIA FACT FILE

PART TWO

NIGERIA: SELF-DETERMINATION AND THE BURDEN OF NATION BUILDING

- **FAILURE OF THE NATION'S LEADERS**
- **DAMAGE ON NATION'S PSYCHE**

CHAPTER FIVE

INDEPENDENCE AND THE BURDEN OF NATION BUILDING

It was obvious, as it would later be seen that the so-called leaders clamoring for independence were not ready for it when it was foisted on them. For the first time, a part of the people's wish was respected when the then Cameroonian part of Nigeria voted against being a part of the contraption called Nigeria. It was unfortunate that it was not decided there and then that the entire country should vote whether they would want to live together as one or go their separate ways. As the full responsibility of leading the nation fell on the agitators for independence when the British opted out in 1960.

The date 1st October 1960 signaled the beginning of a new direction for the nation without definite objectives. The exit of the Europeans also exposed the myopic nature of our leaders in nation building. They had all failed the first true test of leadership where most other African leader like Kwame Nkrumah had succeeded. Not quite three years after the whites had gone that they began to tear the nation further apart in their drive to be ultimate leaders for their own selfish ambitions.

If the truth however must be told on the failure of the first republic, the North had no hand in it. It was the sole responsibility of Dr. Nnamdi Azikiwe and Chief Obafemi Awolowo that it failed. These two from their own history saw themselves as the alpha and the omega of their regional and national politics. They were either the leaders or no one else could lead. To the contrary, the Sarduana was more accommodating of his people's excesses.

He made sure that positions of authority were not exclusively his prerogative. If the Sardauna could reject the position of the prime minister nominating instead, his assistant in Tafawa Balewa for the same position while preferring the lower regional premier, one wonders why Zik and Awolowo would so believe that they could do it better than anyone else. That was the beginning of leadership crisis in Nigeria, nay, in the South.

Secondly the North was never vehement in the fight for independence so if the first republic failed, the North could still easily be exonerated. By the time, the nation was granted self determination, the North knew it was not ready yet it was not also ready to watch the rest of the country leave it behind in the scheme of things. As the South agitated for independence, the North soon joined in the fray in order not to be left out of a nation where its leaders knew it could call the shots.

It was the elections that would expose the shortcomings of our leaders and the nature of nation they were building, it would also expose further the direction to which they were driving the contraption called Nigeria. It was clear that no Nigeria nationalist was a rallying point for all other people. Rather, you have leaders who were rallying points only for their ethnic regions. No Nigerian enjoyed the kind of popularity enjoyed by other great African leaders like Kwame Nkrumah, Jomo Kenyatta, Kenneth Kaunda, Nelson Mandela and the late Samora Machelle. These men were national leaders of true national dispositions rather than the tribal dispositions of our leaders.

Nigeria at independence lacked a true national leader with genuine national interest who would have been a rallying point for the nation and think tank for a prosperous true Federal Republic of Nigeria. Dr. Nnamdi Azikiwe could have fitted a little bit into these shoes, but for lack of clear-cut ideology and an ideal basis for his believes in one true Nigeria. Chief Obafemi Awolowo was more entangled in the struggle for the soul of Yorubaland to focus on national issues as a true national leader despite his clear-cut ideologies of state welfarism.

Sir Ahmadu Bello never pretended that there was any love lost between him and the entire Nigeria, his concern were basically for his people, the Northerners. He would rather let his lieutenant, Sir Abubakar Tafawa Balewa handle matters that concern his party and the contraption called Nigeria. Sir Tafawa Balewa was representing just a sectional interest at the centre and was more of the NPC errand boy to the centre that even the North did not believe would not soon collapse.

The Prime Minister was an errand boy for some feudal lords handling a responsibility too enormous for his burdened shoulder. He simply had no ideology, apart from those taught him by religion and dictated to him from Kaduna and Sokoto. While Awolowo wanted a truly independent nation, his disdain for other sections of the country that he sought to rule stood in his way to achieving that aim for which he lacked a clear cut path to achieving. Others in the union to him would have become second class citizens.

As the struggle for power continued, the Western minorities began to articulate their positions and agitation for self-determination. They evidently saw that they no longer had any future in Awolowo's or Akintola's West.

It was obvious that all was no longer fair in the old arrangement - the lumping together of the minorities of the old Midwest to the West was another mistake by the colonialists. Oba Akenzua, Chief Festus Okotie-Eboh, Chief Dennis Osadebe, Olorogun Marriere and others began the agitation for a Mid-Western State to mature in their time.

The battle for the soul of the nation had become a do-or-die affair between the leaders who presumably had fought to liberate the same soul from the hold of the colonialists. The NCNC and the NPC had begun to see Chief Awolowo's AG as the big threat to their political ambitions. The result was a stop-the-AG-by-all-means necessary dictum that saw a national gang up between the NPC and the NCNC to stop the AG even in the West.

In the elections that followed, the NCNC had fulfilled its promise for the creation of the Mid-Western state not because it believed in the genuine cause of minority agitation but because it sought to divide the home base of the Action Group and make it a minority party in 1963. Thus for the first time, the minorities had their own region. It has to be stated again that this gesture of the NPC-NCNC coalition government was not borne out of good will or sympathy for the minority course but to cut down on the electoral fortunes of the AG and gain on the grudge of the minorities of the area against the AG.

It was clear from the onset that the nation lacked someone with real political clout to make any impression. Voting was patterned along ethnic lines and allegiances were purely on tribal grounds rather than the potential of the candidate. This scenario was to snowball into a major crisis that even the leaders could not manage. Due to tribal mistrust, population figures were altered as each tribe tried to gain numerical advantage over the other. Elections were massively rigged along ethnic lines. Rather than be cohesive, the political class became one loose bunch. Corruption became part of the national order.

It is unfortunate that politicians have begun to loot the nation as far as the early years of nationhood. It is this foundation as laid by the founders of the nation that is today still crippling the nation. It has become so endemic that no one cares to look at its root. Corruption was almost becoming part of the national order. The political class was at each other's throat. This led to mass riots across the nation, looting, murder, and arson became the order of the day as the new nation headed for the brink of collapse.

Political opponents were arrested and thrown into jail at trump-up charges. Chief Obafemi Awolowo fought the battle of his life as he declared himself winner of the Western election against S. L. Akintola who himself was declared winner. Both formed parallel government for the West. Awolowo was arrested and charged with charges of treasonable felony and jailed. The existence of the new nation was greatly threatened. In the North, the Hausas had begun to kill and burn the houses of those they consider infidels in their midst.

The riots that engulfed the nation had been in the West and the Northern regions. These riots were beyond the control of the leaders who watched the nation drift towards civil war in less than six years of independence. In the East, what seemed like agitation for the creation of another region for the minorities lacked merit before the NPC-NCNC government so long as the East was controlled by the NCNC. The politics of the time was that of bitterness, vendetta and ethnicity. Certain reasons could be adduced for the inability of the founding fathers to shoulder the responsibility of statehood after independence;

- Nigeria's independence came from the struggle of political class that were probably disoriented as at that time with the people's wish, because of the colonial mentality that the nation was okay the way it was configured by the colonialist. If it were, Cameroon would have opted to remain in it when it had the chance to make the choice.

- Most of them had been educated outside the country and did not have the time to experience what the likes of Pa Imoudu suffered in terms of racial discrimination and wage disparity.

- The struggles for independence that they claimed to have attained were more of tea conferences in London and Europe. It was thus always negotiation over cup of tea and struggle for ego dominance as was evident in the Nigeria Youth Movement.

- They were never core players in the neo-Negro movements of the time that sought to establish the dignity of the black man as a force for the world. They were but local brigades.

- Their fight against colonialism was not issue oriented. It was more of academic and image boosting exercise. They were not grass-roots mobilizers.

- As it became evident, at independence, they were more interested in taking over from the colonialist just to fill the vacuum than provide exemplary leadership for the people.
- The so-called founding fathers cannot lay claims to having led the people in mass protest against any colonial laws outside protests against the colonial constitutions as did the Aba women riots of 1928/1929, the Pa Imoudu labor protests etc.

Perhaps, one factor responsible for the inability of the founding fathers to build a virile nation after independence was the fact that their patience was never tried. The Nigerian nationalist did not have to lay down his life in the prison of the colonialists like Jomo Kenyatta, Kenneth Kaunda, Nelson Mandela, Robert Mugabe and thousands who warded off the colonialists with their blood. The Nigeria struggle was usually a discussion over cups of tea. And when independence came on a platter of gold it was another form of colonialism, only this time, of Nigeria by Nigerians.

The Europeans did not get greedy in Nigeria like they did in other countries where the land and beautiful water fronts in choice areas of the country were appropriated like they did in Zambia, South Africa, Algeria, Kenya and other parts of Africa. Nigerians did not have to fight a war like the Americans did to liberate themselves from colonialism. These factors underscore the seriousness of the leaders to be truly national in their approach to issues.

Going back into the records of the founding fathers, the first attempt at mass protest that touched on the grassroots was against the Richardson Constitution in

1946 in which they claimed Nigerians were not consulted. The protest yielded the first major consultation with Nigerians from the grassroots, the villages, district, provinces and regional levels. A lot of conferences were held in which the people made their inputs on how they would be governed.

The ethnic groups were represented while the minority report from the conference was given less attention. This consultation yielded the 1951 McPherson Constitution with a revision in 1954 in Lagos and London. This then produced the Lyttleton Constitution. If this kind of consultation had been held for the ethnic nationalities before independence to determine the basis of their coexistence, perhaps the nation would have faired better in over fifty years of co-existence as a sovereign nation.

While other leaders like Kwame Nkrumah, Jomo Kenyatta etc succeeded in building their nation into one virile and cohesive nation, Nigeria leaders failed in their leadership duty. The convenient argument has been the fact that Nigeria is too large and too complex to be governed like these other nations. India is a larger community of nations; Indira Ghandi was able to wield the nation together as did Jawaral Nehru at independence.

When the experiment of the British to wield strange bedfellows together in India failed, Pakistan and India went their separate ways at independence in 1948. Since then both nations had developed competitive spirits. Both nations have been developing to attain self-sufficiency out of the fear of one dominating the other. Another reason Nigeria leaders failed could be that they did not experience the often-extreme aspect of colonialism where the subjects are treated less humanly.

84

They were thus not skilful at arousing the sentiment of the people across ethnic divide.

At independence the political class could not conduct proper elections. Results of the elections into the Federal Houses were massively rigged in favour of the ruling party. The leaders engaged each other in free political assassination, thuggery, riots etc. Census result of 1962-1964 was massively falsified to influence the increased electoral fortunes of the ruling parties. Looting of treasury, bribery and corruption went unabated. The Action Group had broken up in its domain between Awolowo and Akintola. By 1965, the nation was heading for total collapse.

The leaders fought more to keep themselves in power than they actually fought for the interest of the nation. They fought to remain relevant in power sharing both within their region and at the centre that they failed to realize that the nation was drifting to the path of total collapse. Seeds of discord were sown among their followers within the regions each controlled.

As it could be seen the so called leaders of the nation had led the nation through five years of mystery, bribery, looting, murder, thuggery, forgery, kick backs, ethnic mistrust, and religious bickering. The chance to build a true Nigeria nation after the British had gone was squandered. No one thought of the past and then tried to work out a present and a future for the nation among the nationalists. The responsibility of statehood was too heavy on them that they lost focus. They prepared the way for the eventuality – the entrance of the military.

Thus the search for the building of a true Nigeria where all are equal, where one holds another in high esteem, where one respects another as equal citizen, where one can freely chooses where to live, where one can decide to be citizen of any part therefore and not be intimidated, where one will not be discriminated against based on religion, where one will not be afraid of a hopeless future, where one can indeed be proud – continues. Then enter the military boys.

CHAPTER SIX

<u>THE NZEOGWU'S COUP EXAMINED</u>

The most controversial figure in today's Nigeria remains Major Chukwuma Kaduna Nzeogwu, the man that led the first military coup in Nigeria. He is a figure as controversial as Nigeria. He in some people inspires awe, while to some others he is a villain. To some he is a national hero deserving of national recognition while to others his memory is better confined to the dustbin of history never to be exhumed again. Irrespective of what view or opinion one holds, the fact remains that Nzeogwu came, lived and abruptly reordered the course of our national history.

What Nzeogwu did in 1965 was not an ambition exclusive to him and his collaborators as Sir Ahmadu Bello had already seen the future and had begun to prepare the North for it. It is commonly said that he encouraged Northerners to go into the army as a measure to check the incursion of the South in politics and counter their quest for western education. This was after a military coup had taken place in a nearby West African country.

For the likes of young officers from the North who had joined the army from 1957, Ahmadu Bello must have been seen as a true leader encouraging his people, the Northerners to join the military to prepare them for the eventuality. But for someone like Nzeogwu from records available, the Sardauna was one the people propagating politics of ethnicism, like the other founding fathers.

Nzeogwu's role in reshaping the political landscape of the country has been well documented by his friend and three times leader of the country Chief (Rtd. General) Olusegun Obasanjo in his book titled "NZEOGWU". Obasanjo fell short of calling him a national hero. The question is Nzeogwu a hero or villain?

Bearing in mind that Nzeogwu did not rule the country despite the coup, is it still enough for one to go ahead and conclude that he was a hero, villain, or a tribalist? Was his purported coming aimed to nip the killing, looting, arson, bribery and political bickering in the bud right timed? Does the fact that the major players in the coup were Ibos make him a tribalist on a mission of enthroning the tribal dominance of Ibos? Was the killing of ministers deliberately one sided or selective to eliminate politicians of non-Ibo extraction?

First and foremost, Chief Olusegun Obasanjo, a former military ruler and civilian president of Nigeria of Yoruba extraction had this to say about the person and believes of the man Nzeogwu, his friend, as he knew him. Quoting from his book "NZEOGWU"

> *"Chukwuma had a dream of great Nigeria that is a force to reckon with in the world, not through ineffective political rhetoric but through purposeful and effective action. He had a dream of an order and orderly nation through a disciplined society. He also dreamt of a country where national interest overrides self, sectional or tribal interest. He wanted a country where a person's ability, output, merit and*

productivity would determine his social and economic progress, rather than political and ethnic considerations.

He had a dream of a country free of graft and greed. He believed in virtues and values other than mere acquisition, glorification and adulation of material wealth. He dreamt of a nation where social justice and economic interest of its citizens will not be subjugated to foreign control and manipulation. He believed in the ability of the black man.

He had a dream of a country where everybody is everybody else's keeper, irrespective of language, tribe, religion, or region. He lived for thirty years, the last two of which he spent trying to achieve his dream for the country of his birth and the country he loved. He failed in the realization of his dream and became victim of that dream. But he left a permanent imprint on the country as well as lesson for all Nigerians to learn".

If the above were a perfect description of what the man actually stood for instead of another ambitious gun trotting mad military man, then he probably would be the last hero of his generation. One will thus be tempted to conclude that the coup was not just an ambitious quest for power by the fact that Nzeogwu had been entrusted with the nation's military arsenal. If we take the description on its face value against the background of the situation in Nigeria at the time, then Obasanjo stopped short of calling Nzeogwu a national hero. Still, was Nzeogwu ever a hero?

What about the allegation that the coup was designed to eliminate only leaders from certain sections of the country? And that the coup was actually a one tribe conspiracy. A look at the major players would give this last impression. The five majors apart from one were all Ibos. But is this reason enough to conclude that the coup was designed against the North? From the accounts of the players who had survived, this was not meant to be but is their words enough?

A look at the major casualties of the coup would reveal that the coup was not actually designed against the North. The South-West had more major casualties in both civilian and military casualty viz.: Brigadier Ademulegun, Col. Shodehinde, Lt. Col. Pam, Mrs. Ademulegun, Lt. Col. Unegbe, Chief Okotie-Eboh, Chief S. L. Akintola etc as against Brig. Maimalari, Col. Mohammed, Sir Abubakar Tafawa Balewa, Sir Ahmadu Bello etc.

Unfortunately as it would appear, the Ibos had little or no casualties as against the other ethnic groups, this made the coup seem selective in execution. If the accounts of the coup are anything to go by, then it would seem that the other collaborators in the coup suddenly realized they owe tribal allegiance to their Ibo leaders, which stopped them from carrying out the operation to its letter. Or may be they suddenly did not want to share the dream of Nzeogwu with him again realizing that they have to dominate the other tribes.

According to Obasanjo, Nzeogwu became a victim of his own vision which as it seem was not shared by the other collaborators who had under flimsy excuses bungled the so-called revolution and taken to their heels for fear of being reprimanded. Despite Nzeogwu's vision, was his action the best option? Nzeogwu's action had changed the course of the history of the nation. Is he then a villain? If he were a villain, so were other coup-plotters that came after him.

If he were a usurper, so was every military man that ever ruled the country. If he were a tribalist, worse still were those that came after him. If he were a murderer, then the others that came after him also were. Whatever negative thing Nzeogwu had been adjudged to be, those other coup-plotters that came after him also were. Nzeogwu erroneously believed he was coming to salvage the nation so were the other military rulers who instead had plunged the country into deeper crises.

Nzeogwu never had the opportunity to actualize his own dreams unlike the other villains. They had the opportunities to set the nation on the right footing but chose to bungle them for their own selfish dreams. Rather than sing songs of progress and unity, it had been retrogression and divisiveness. Nigeria had been a mystery working and moving slowly and drifting away from values that should bind as a nation to values that coerces us to live together not willingly but grudgingly.

The people live in constant fear of one another as a people forced into a union to which they were not willing to be bound. They do not live as coequals but as conquered subordinates that must be subjected to the dictates of their conquerors. This is the daily dilemma of the average Nigeria. He feels subjected like a slave to his own environment. As it would seem he has lost faith in the nation. This did not start today; it started right from the very beginning when Lagos became a colony in 1850 and later Calabar.

Then to the time that the country was wrongly amalgamated in 1914 without regard for the sovereign will of the ethnic nationals that constituted it. The colonialists ruled as if they were the conquerors and liberators of a jungle peopled by half apes and half Homo sapiens not deserving of any right. Their concerns were not for the people but for the resources in the jungle from which they fed their home industries. This tradition of the colonialists was entrenched by the rulers after independence and perpetrated in the military tradition that began the period of internal colonialism as started by Nzeogwu's so-called vision in the tradition of coups.

Even in the pre-colonial Nigeria, when kingdoms conquered one another, the conquered territories were allowed to live within the dictates of their own custom and political institutions. They were only subjected to the payment of tributes to the working of the over all objectives of the empire. Among the conquered territories, men were allowed to realize their full potentials by rising to position of prominence.

This was why in the Sokoto Caliphate anyone irrespective of his indigent community could become the Sardauna. In Oyo Empire, anyone could become the Aare Onakankanfo irrespective of the community he comes from within the empire. Slave boys like the Jaja of Opobo could become king irrespective of being stranger in the land. This is the nature of society that Nigerian leaders have failed to build.

The dreams of Nzeogwu as purported by Chief Olusegun Obasanjo was lacking in Nigeria right from the first day of independence. There not been real physical,

92

infrastructural as well as human development in Nigeria. Most claimed gains in the economy existing only in the pages of newspapers and has never translated into good lives for the people in general. Poverty has been the bane of the society.

The leaders lacked real political will to move the nation forward economically. To make any economic progress, there must first be a political will that entrenches fairness and truly rewards hard work irrespective of ethnic, religious or political affiliations. A political will that must recognize the truth and seek to protect it, a will that must care for the betterment of all and meet our future overall objective. A political will that seeks not the welfare of self above the collective, but making the welfare of the collective the personal goal to be achieved.

This is the basis of building a strong, united and virile nation. This requires that all falsehood that belies the foundation of the nation must be dug into and corrected. Then the people will of their own accord decide to move the nation along the path of common destiny. The nation does not need to be pulled in different directions by the discordant tunes of tribal, religious and ethnic jingoes sang by a drowning political class, whose only concern are themselves and their household, who also very soon abandons the land in the ruins they have engineered.

Nzeogwu's coup was the beginning of another long year of waste and lack of visionary leadership. The military that came to replace the leaders were the most ill-equipped for the job of political leadership. Nzeogwu who had the vision of the revolution that he envisaged, could not carry it out to the letter, as it was foiled by his so-called kinsmen who had lost sight of the vision. It was leadership without the participation of the visionary. The nation had begun to head towards the mother of all crises, compounded by the grandiose vision of Nzeogwu.

It must be stated that Nzeogwu, himself actually lacked foresight and true dream. His method of achieving his dream was a crime against humanity. He was first and foremost a disillusioned young man in a hurry to keep a date with destiny and history. The price of his action was civil war and years of military wastefulness for the nation and a tinkering with an arrangement that would have sorted out itself.

If the truth however must be told, the truth is that Nzeogwu is a villain, no matter what dream of the nation he may have been said to have. His ambition altered the course of history for the nation and genuine path to desired change. The creation of the Mid-Western Region would have marked the beginning of the path to true federalism and a virile nation. The crises were means of change that would have sorted out itself politically.

At least, further crisis into which Nzeogwu's action had plunged the nation has not generated any good ideas on moving the nation forward. The crises of the first political era would have generated ideas at moving the nation forward after a period of political inactivity. Then the nation would have renegotiated its existence to further strengthen the union. This could have been achieved only politically not militarily as envisaged by Nzeogwu. While the leaders may have derailed in handling the nation's affairs, it was not reason enough for Nzeogwu's self-ambition to set the nation back as it were to the dark age of force and brutality when the only thing the early men knew was coercion.

94

Had Nzeogwu kept his calm or discarded the uniform to woo the electorate on his vision and not allow the push of his gun barrel drive him into a coup, it is not doubtful that solutions would have been found round the civil war of waste. Nigeria would have sorted things out herself and correct the problems. Nzeogwu had no moral justification to have led a mutiny against the very nation from whose resources he trained as a military officer and whose interest he swore to protect. He was indeed a victim of his own ambition not his dreams. Dreams are often achieved but ambitions are hard especially when they are inimical to a people's progress. As Nzeogwu, so were the other military leaders of Nigeria that came after him. They had all sinned against the nation.

None of them had any moral justification to rule the nation with the fist of barrel, looting and improvising the people as they did. They are all guilty of the sins of Nzeogwu and need to apologize to the nation for their contribution to the destruction of the nation.

CHAPTER SEVEN

<u>NIGERIA LEADERSHIP AFTER THE FIRST COUP TILL 1999</u>

The essence of the coup of January was to change a corrupt and decaying order but what we got from it was a set of gluttonous and short-sighted leaders. The beneficiaries of the Nzeogwu led mutiny did not seem to agree with Nzeogwu that something was wrong with the system. They simply refused to catch the vision of the visionaries. Major General Aguiyi Ironsi picked up leadership like a child walking into his mother's kitchen to pick a plate of food. The child cares less if there is anything like table manner. The child least knows what has gone into preparing the meal.

Major General Ironsi was the first Nigerian General of the postcolonial army. Yet again he became Nigeria's first military ruler. What great role destiny seemed to have for him! He became the Head of State on a platter of gold. He did not ask for it, he did not plan for it, neither did he attempt to have it. It just fell on his laps. He found that ruling Nigeria was a different ball game from being a commander in the army. Politics was not part of his training. Within six months, he had lost control of the whole situation.

Aguiyi Ironsi found he was not the solution to the problem of Nigeria. It was much more than the vision of Nzeogwu and more than the leadership of a military man. He had no solution to the crises that had engulfed the nascent nation in the twilight of her independence. He was too myopic to think that the Nigerian army had been immune to the problems of the entire society.

He had thought that the Nigeria society was the same military institution he joined as a young officer. He believed he was pledging allegiance to the nation. He forgot to see that the politicians who had begun to entrench tribalism in the military had infiltrated the institution. The very problem of the federation consumed the new leader who in the first place had no business in leadership. His was a political misadventure and military suicide.

The Northerners had become more vicious and more antagonistic towards other tribes, a situation, which the then head of state could not control. A section of the country had become laws onto themselves and if it were possible would have preferred the nation broken. Before the new man at the helms of affairs settled down, he was hurriedly swept out of the office as the real owners came to have it.

As Ironsi settled down to the realities on ground, he was swept off by the very same crisis that had led him by fate's cruel way into the state house. Junior officers in the same rank group as Nzeogwu who seemed more on revenge mission of ethnic cleansing toppled him. It was clear from the onset that the Nzeogwu's coup would produce a counter coup sooner or later; only, it came sooner than it seemed Ironsi expected. Ironsi's only achievement in office before he was butchered was the promulgation in May 1966 of the slavery decree, called the Unitary Decree 34, which gave all powers to the centre.

The counter coup was purely a Northern affair led by General Yakubu Gowon. Much senior officers had to be retired and he was hurriedly promoted to make him most senior officer. Theirs was a coup of retaliation. This much had been admitted by General Gowon himself that the butchering coup of July 29, 1966 that he led was in retaliation for the perceived wrongs of Nzeogwu's coup against the North. It was the coup that consolidated on the gains of the North over the South and thus begun the era of systematic enslavement of the South to the North.

General Gowon who became the leader of Nigeria after Major General Ironsi had been murdered cut the picture of someone who was the opposite of what was described as the believes of Nzeogwu. He probably would be nowhere near leadership if the slogan of monolithic North had not worked perfectly well in the psyche of the average Northerner. It was obvious that Gowon throughout his tenure as the head of state did not fully come to terms with leadership. The young man simply did not know what it meant to be the head of state of a nation like Nigeria.

The coup was a repetition of the Nzeogwu commando display of unintelligent bravado as young officers of the Nigeria Army saddled themselves with leadership of the nation to which they had sworn allegiance to defend. They threw this allegiance in the face of the nation and usurp the process of national political evolution. The responsibility was something they did not prepare for neither were they trained to do. The result was the civil war that resulted in the waste of lives.

The nation was plunged into an avoidable civil war in less than ten years of independence. The military boys attempted to solve political problems in the military method of subdue-and-conquer-them. The civil war brought three years of misery to the civil populace in Nigeria. Though Gowon declared a No Victor, No Vanquished situation but the truth was that some people had been victorious while others had been vanquished.

Despite the fact that the head of state had declared the end of the civil (1967-1970) period of reconstruction, reconciliation, and rehabilitation period, it was glaring that someone's ego had been hurt. Since then, the Ibos have become second class citizens in a country that was reeking of the decay of the past.

The events that culminated in the civil war could have been averted. The crises in which Chief Emeka Odumegwu Ojukwu, the leader of the seceding Biafra and General Gowon were the major players, could have been the right opportunity to reconsider the basis of our national coexistence. As it was, Ojukwu seemed to be so much in a hurry, blinded by the tribal heroism that had become the bane of the Nigeria society. Both leaders who did not know what leadership entails were led by youthful exuberance in their quest for political relevance on the terrain where they had no business being.

The prospect of a new Biafra, independent of the Nigeria Republic excited him so much that he had begun to see himself as the champion of the Ibo course as had been represented by the old political class. All caution were thus thrown to the wind in pursuant of a meaningless course that probably did have the blessings of the majority of the people. The result is that the Ibos are still bearing the psychological effect of having to lose in the war.

Chief Obafemi Awolowo who found favour in the new regime and should have used the opportunity to begin the negotiation for a true Nigeria of their dream would rather threaten Gowon with the secession of the Yorubas should Ojukwu be allowed to go with Biafra. In haste, rather than consolidate on the gains of Aburi negotiation (the West had conveniently aligned with the North to stop the secession bid of the East), Ojukwu began a hurried aggression with an ill prepared military against a more professional Nigerian Army, a move that was dearly paid for. His action in the past has turned the Ibos into second class citizens in the nation's political equation today.

It was obvious that if the Ibos had been allowed full self-determination within the nation or outside the federation, the Ibo nationality would have grown in technological potentials that would have seen that Nigeria grows above her contemporaries in sub-Sahara Africa. The skill exhibited by the Biafra engineers during the civil war has, thirty years later become extinct due to the lack of foresight of the bunch of leaders that imposed themselves on the nation since independence.

Despite being one of the three tripods, the Ibos seem to have completely lost out in the national equation. They are completely viewed with distrust by the other ethnic nationalities. Even the regime of Gowon that declared a no victor, no vanquished verdict could not live up to its declaration. Biafra soldiers were never fully integrated into the Nigeria Army. The people were never rehabilitated; they were treated like the devil.

The Gowon era was the period of consolidation of Northern interest. The Arewa boys began to reposition themselves for the role of leading the nation like another conquered territory only this time by the Sokoto caliphate or descendants of Usman Dan Fodio. As it would seem, state creation became an act to gain the favour of the populace. The aim was to make them look away from the aberration perpetrated by the incursion of the military into the nation's political life.

Though, the people welcomed it, the task of state creation was an act meant to break the loyalty of the Eastern minority to Ojukwu regime. They were not done because the regime was trying to yield to the dictates of popular opinion. The military institution after the war became discriminatory. Issue of employment and promotion became tied to tribal origin, god-fatherism, and religious inclination. Military career became the exclusive preserve of the Northerners.

The reconciliation in Gowon's post-civil war Nigeria was rather mere lip service than action, as no attempt was made towards true reconciliation. Gowon bungled the opportunity to truly put Nigeria aright, despite the economic boost that came with crude oil. His regime killed the national economy more than any other regime in the nation's history. The people became slaves of imperialism as his regime lacked foresight for true national development.

Rather than work out programmes for the nation's sustainable development, he completely killed the agricultural sector. Worse still, the nation became so rich the insane leader of a sick nation could do nothing with the nation's wealth than go and pay the bills of other nations. The nation under Gowon was so rich that it lost focus of future developmental programmes. As the nation grew richer, this wealth became the albatross to good leadership. The source of the wealth decayed steadily as the gluttonic desires of the leaders were fed upon. The same nation is so deep in debt today with the leaders so rich that their wealth is more than the total debt profile of the nation.

It was obvious that Gowon was driving the nation towards another catastrophe, a catastrophe that could be worse than the civil war. He was leading the nation on a path that would be worse than the colonial enslavement of the ethnic nationals. He had no goals and his regime had no national objectives for proper development neither was he even versed in the peculiar nature of the problem that confronted the nation. He was satisfied with being the leader of the giant of Africa. A position he wanted to keep forever.

The same accusations leveled against the civilians by the military were the same accusations leveled against the Gowon administration. His removal brought much relieves to Nigerians who felt that he had overstayed his welcome. The coming of General Murtala Mohammed was a big relief to Nigerians. He came with so much zeal and desire to rid the system of the corruption that had become endemic in the system. He exhibited enough political will to correct the wrongs within the system. His measures were popular as well as unpopular.

He was tolerated due to the fact that he set the timetable for military disengagement from the state house to the barracks. It was in the pursuit of this goal that he was assassinated and his regime cut short by another ambitious young officer Col. Sukar Dimka. Murtala's regime lasted less than twelve months. Though the head of state was killed but the coup against him failed as leadership fell on the deputy to the late Gen. Murtala Mohammed.

Fate foisted another leader on the nation in the person of General Olusegun Obasanjo who was the second in command to the assassinated head of state. The best that this regime was remembered for were the handing over to an elected government and the operation feed the nation (OFN) programme. OFN was aimed at salvaging the dead agricultural sector. He is also known for the popular land use act that further annexed all Nigeria land and resource. Petroleum resources bearing land became extension of the government property without annexing the people while farm lands remain the properties of the community in which they domicile. He kept annexing everything petroleum including foreign oil businesses in Nigeria without annexing the foreigners as well.

In his first time out, the head of state was too busy preparing to hand over to note the deviation from the programme of his erstwhile boss Gen. Murtala Mohammed in the fight against corruption. The scourge had crept back into the system that it seemed the military rulers were in a hurry to steal as much as they could before they go back to the barracks. The nation's vault was thrown open to the looters who not under the seeming control of the leader who was in a hurry to depart.

His deputy, the late Major General Yar'Adua amassed enough to later build the most formidable political organization in the nation. He made very good use of his political machinery to reach the grassroots in his bid to become the president of Nigeria. His organization cut across ethnic boundaries with basic support from the grassroots. Yar'Adua was probably the first detribalized politician the nation had ever seen. He was the first politician without ethnic or religious prejudice. He had the nation as his constituency.

General Obasanjo retired from the nation's top job to a life of more affluence than he could handle in 1979 after handing over to an elected civilian government after a questionable and doctored election process. His regime produced a new set of millionaire generals within and outside of the Nigeria Army. Operation Feed the Nation; an official agricultural program initiated by the General became operation feed Ota Farms, the general's personal business. The Generals that were left in the military as well as those that retired with him became very wealthy as they handed over to incompetent politicians to continue the tradition of looting.

The regime of General Olusegun Obasanjo was the first to witness a wave of students' demonstration in the 'Ali Must Go' saga. His transition programme brought back the old brigades, with a few new breeds. At the end, five political parties reminiscent of the political parties of the 1960s were formed in readiness for the 1979 elections.

Chief Obafemi Awolowo became the leader as well as the presidential candidate of the Yoruba dominated Unity Party of Nigeria (UPN), Dr. Nnamdi Azikiwe became the leader as well as the presidential candidate of the Igbo dominated Nigeria Peoples Party (NPP). The other parties were the Great Nigeria Peoples Party (GNPP) of Alhaji Ibrahim Waziri, Peoples Redemption Party (PRP) of Mallam Aminu Kano and the National Party of Nigeria (NPN) led by Chief Akinloye with Alhaji Shehu Shagari as presidential candidate. The National Advance Party (NAP) of Dr. Tunji Braithwaite came later.

It was not surprising that the founding fathers lost to a political neophyte like Shehu Shagari of the NPN even though the election results were questionable. NPN was the only party that was more national in outlook. The others had ethnic coloration, as the leaders became cult figures to their followers. It was obvious that the so-called founding fathers committed political suicide in their second incursion into the political terrain. Nigerian preferred trying new hands to the old brigades who were the fathers of ethnic politics in the nation.

Dr. Nnamdi Azikiwe seems to have realized only too late that there was wisdom in Chief Obafemi Awolowo's proposal for an alliance. Both men had assumed cult personality in politics that stepping down for each other in the alliance to defeat the rampaging NPN would mean conceding political superiority. In the first republic, an AG-NCNC alliance perhaps could have caused the nation less trouble than the NCNC-NPC alliance that almost tore the nation apart.

While the two could not work out their differences, the North consolidated on political gains arising from the ego war between the two giants. This led to Shagari victory at the polls. The North had come to realize that the only way to even their disadvantage was holding on to political power since the South had become much empowered economically. Thus Shagari defeated the giants narrowly in the 1979 general elections.

If the NPN narrowly won the 1979 election, the 1983 election was a clean sweep of the polls by the same party though fraught with allegations of rigging. The party made a clean sweep of even the domains of the fathers in the East and West to show that even the people were becoming weary of the fathers' style of ethnic politics. It was a hurricane NPN that swept the polls in 1983.

Alhaji Shehu Shagari was to continue the 'born to rule' agenda of the North. He was to lead the nation into an era of unabated corruption. A new idiom replaced the kick back of the first republic. Ten percent became the new norm in public life. Except for its democratic nature, it was another government of waste that began to lead Nigeria deeper into poverty, continuing in the tradition of the system. As the party and state officials became richer, the country got poorer.

As it would seem, the question of ethnic minority and the nation's unity is always substituted for representative governance. Representative participation is often assumed to have taken care of minority fears with the major tribes often using their numbers to muzzle the minorities. Democracy has never allayed these fears; rather they become more entrenched, popping up at every opportunity.

The Shagari regime despite the nation's earning in the oil sector declared that the nation was broke and had to begin the campaign for austerity measures. As the nation sank deeper into poverty, the NPN chieftains got richer. Government officials embezzled both money earned and borrowed. Leaders in a hurry to empty its vault drain all it's wealth and left it groping invaded the nation. It was another four years of national waste with a visionless government.

As the second term approached after a first four years of waste, Shagari was too busy trying to outdo the old gladiators on their tribal grounds to make him look like a new national hero to notice that he had driven the nation worse off than 1966. His green revolution had grown brown and lacked the greenery to give it foliage. He had indeed become colour blind to see the looting being perpetrated by his lieutenants and co-drivers in the doomed regime.

The Shagari regime became rather preoccupied with dealing with religious, ethnic and political riots. The entire nation was embroiled in ethnic distrust as the ethnic nationals were at each other's throat. The North once again made it abundantly clear that it was the colonial master while the South was its vassal state. The then governor of Bendel State, Late Prof. Ambrose Ali spent more time in court fighting the injustice of the federal arrangement in revenue sharing formula.

The re-election of the president was marred with great protests from across the country. It ranged from intra-party bitterness to riots across the country against the rigging as perpetrated by the ruling party. The same crisis that engulfed the nation at independence reared its head again. The alliance between the so-called progressives could not work out against the ruling NPN as the fathers, Chief Obafemi Awolowo and Dr. Nnamdi Azikiwe would not shift grounds on who leads the alliance.

The political class had once more demonstrated that they were more interested in their personal ambitions than in the progress of the nation. The election had already generated enough crises to once more spur other anti-progressive elements within the army to pseudo-patriotism in the duty for fatherland. It was not long after that these elements came rolling out their guns from the barracks in the name of saving the nation from the brink of collapse due to the various riots, murder, maiming, arson going on across the nation. Just like Balewa did not see it coming so also did Shagari not see it coming, only that this time, the President was lucky to be spared his life.

On 31, December 1983, Shagari was shoved aside, barely three months after his swearing-in for a second term, in a coup masterminded by General Ibrahim Babangida and announced by General Sanni Abacha. General Buhari emerged as the Head of State. Buhari's regime was that of slaves and master. Nigerians were his slaves while he was the master. He never hid his disdain for the South and other religion outside Islam. His second in command was a Northerner and a Muslim. He had no regard for decorum.

He made it clear that he was never to be opposed. He had no patience for due course of law. He stopped short of introducing the Sharia Law into the national polity. He brought decrees to muzzle the press and instant death for offenders of certain crimes even before the court of law pronounces such guilty. His regime had reduced Nigerians to beggars as they must queue up every Friday for what his regime had termed 'essential commodities', which only his government had the prerogative to import and distribute to workers.

Nigerians will not forget the decrees 2, 4 and 20 in a hurry, for the Buhari's regime, no Nigerian dared to challenge his excesses, he was tending towards a refined Idi Amin in Nigeria. He was the Lord of the jungle or the Sultan of Nigeria. His rather short stay in power was packed full of activities that Nigerians will not forget in a hurry for the generations to come.

Decree 2 gave the Chief of Staff Supreme Headquarters the power to detain anyone without trial for up to six months and Decree 4 banned journalists from reporting or publishing any information that is considered embarrassing to any government official. Decree 20 imposed death sentence on drug peddlers who were tried in military tribunals, rather than regular courts. Promptly, Buhari's tribunal condemned three young men - Lawal Ojuolape(30), Bernard Ogedengbe (29) and Bartholomew Owoh (26) to death and had them executed despite a deluge of pleas nationally and internationally to spare them.

It was obvious that Buhari's coup was not against the ruling Shehu Shagari regime but against the opposition and against Nigerians. It was as if the oppositions were the ones that made Shagari a mistake to have happened to Nigeria. Opposition figures like late Adekunle Ajasin were thrown into jail despite being declared not corrupt by Buhari's tribunals. The late Ambrose Alli, Bola Ige, Jim Nwobodo, Alex Ekweme, Bisi Onabanjo and so on languished in Buhari's jail while Shagari enjoyed a five star treatment. Tai Solarin's only crime for going to jail was that he distributed leaflets in street corners. Most governors from the South languished in Buhari's jail while worse northern governors walk free or were given five star treatments like Shagari.

Soldiers took over the market places to loot and sell wares for market women at Buhari's fixed prices. Nigerians were publicly flogged like the Northern cows in what he termed the War Against Indiscipline (WAI). The average Nigerian had lost his self-dignity under him. Politicians were put behind bars in what turned out to be a selective persecution of perceived enemies most especially Southern politicians and dissenting Northern politicians.

Buhari had no regard for the nation's configuration of multi-ethnicity and religious secularity. Nigerian's were bunch of cows from his native Daura town to be whipped and flogged into line. He was indeed a representation of the Northern oligarchy and was willing to maintain that at all cost. He was a staunch believer in the Northern domination of the South. This he showed in his words and actions while in and out of power. He turned Nigerians into garden keepers as they must come out every Saturday to clean the streets and tend the gardens with his goons going round to flog anyone not observing it.

He had shelved the duty of the government to provide a functioning system for Nigerians that would ensure clean and conducive environment. He turned everyone into street cleaners while creating street urchins in WAI brigades, in the name of War Against Indiscipline. He encouraged nothing like infrastructural development except the payment of debt that his Northern brother had incurred for the nation through massive looting of the treasury.

It was obvious that Nigerians barely tolerated the General. Their patience was stretched to the limits; more so, he said he had no political timetable. He had come to sit on the throne of his forefathers like Gowon and Shagari before him, the throne that no one else had the right to aspire to except he was of the same ethnic background and of the same religious affiliation as Buhari. The stance of Buhari and his deputy on national issues were myopic and it was obvious they were never going to last long on the sit.

The coming of General Ibrahim Badamosi Babangida on the 26th of August 1985 was the first coup that was highly applauded by Nigerians who were too glad to be relieved of the Buhari burden. Of all the military leaders that ever ruled Nigeria, Babangida seem the only military leader that had been long prepared for the job he expected he would one day have. He had been part of most coups in Nigeria until he became the military president. Without prejudice his regime seem to have been more focused than all other regimes that came before him, in terms of physical, human and economic programmes.

He rode on the crest of populist programmes to win the heart of Nigerians from the onset of his administration. His administration was the best ever-assembled in Nigeria history, with the most popular, accomplished and intelligent Nigerians serving in his regime. He made Nigerians part of his administration from its inception and sought views in matters that affect the generality of the nation. The fervor of the administration became lost as soon as Nigerians began to see the true nature of the man Babangida.

His orchestrated moves to include Nigerians in his programmes began to fail as Nigerians began to sense that there was something wrong in the administration of Babangida. He had within six years, used and dumped the most brilliant Nigerians soiling them with the oil of corruption for which his regime became known to such unprecedented level unknown of all the regimes before him. Compared with the others before him, his regime was also the best in terms of rural development with the better life for rural women programme anchored by his wife, late Miriam Babangida.

The suppressed fear and ethnic mistrust began to rear its head under him as riots, religious and ethnic bellowed against some of his unpopular programmes. He began to introduce stopgap measures to solving national problems as Nigerians completely lost the confidence they had initially reposed in him. Settlement became official parlance in public circles. Crime rose to unabated level. New crimes like the 419, drug abuse and drug peddling became rampant under IBB's administration. Nigerians suddenly threw caution to the wind and launched into new levels of criminal activities.

Under him the national question of coexistence of the ethnic nationalities assumed a new dimension after the attempted coup of 1990. Major Gideon Orkar in the coup announced the excision of the North-North region from the rest of the country. His was the first major bold step at bringing the ethnic nationals to a round table to negotiate the basis of their coexistence. He had announced that they should come to negotiate their coming back to the nation if they so wished.

This coup was as a result of the bitterness against the injustice in the configuration of the nation and its dominance by a single region. The nation had witnessed a lot of riots in the way national affairs were being manipulated. The attempt at enlisting the nation into the OIC (Organization of Islamic Countries) and declare Islam as a State religion to give the impression that the nation was a single religious state was a case in point. Though there were various denials by those in authority but it was part of the ethnic and religious distrust between the regions and their people.

The Gideon Orkar's coup was a bloody one. Officers from mainly the minority ethnic groups of the nation led it. At the end of the day, the coup failed. Nigeria and the minorities had lost a lot of their best officers in the army. The implication also was the hurried relocation of the capital city of the nation to Abuja from Lagos. At the end of the coup, no one deemed it necessary to address the basis of the coup and redress certain ills in the contraption that was foisted on the people of Nigeria.

This era also witnessed the beginning of the great decay that would creep into the tertiary education. Education at all levels witnessed unprecedented strikes at every level. The school system was virtually comatose between 1990 and 1999. The North-South dichotomy had become so entrenched in the system that the country was barely holding together on hope by some divine arrangement. Military and brutal force had to be used to keep the nation in check. One hope however, kept Nigerians together, the hope that the nation would soon see a change in governance to democratically elected one from the military junta.

The Babangida political timetable seems an endless circle by the time it began. The timetable had to be adjusted severally, either by some deliberate dubious intentions or due to some genuine circumstances. His regime gave impetus to the activities of the human right organizations as well as various environmental organizations. The nation experimented with the unpopular Structural Adjustment Programme that was violently rejected by Nigerians in the late 1980s.

The regime, which initially seemed focus on implementation of programmes, had completely lost focus by 1990. This was the period that the political timetable had overshadowed all other things. The transition programme had tasked the patience of Nigerians after various elections had been annulled; political parties formed by Nigerians were rejected. Two new parties were foisted on Nigerians, and these political organizations became government parastatal.

Various electoral options were implemented ranging from zero-party, option A4, open-secret ballot system, secret ballot systems, etc. Each of the options became obsolete as soon they had been implemented and a new one manufactured from the political strategists. In all, each of the systems had cost the nation several billions of Naira to implement. It was indeed a period of waste.

At the initial stage it would seem that the two parties formed for Nigerians was done along regional lines, as forces from the South saw themselves more in the SDP (Social Democratic Party) and the Northerners align themselves in the NRC (Nigeria Republican Party). Voting in the elections was basically along the regions for both parties. This trend however changed as the nation approached the presidential elections. The Northern masses seem to have suddenly realized that even their feudal lords had misdirected them for too long using the slogan of regionalism and religion.

It was obvious that the Northern oligarchy never expected the outcome of the elections in 1992. It became clear from the result that even the North had rejected the shackles of oppressions, poverty, and ignorance from the feudal oligarchy. The North for once shelved the toga of perpetual ignorance, and threw aside the card of religion often played by their leaders.

Chief M. K. O. Abiola, a Muslim running on the ticket of SDP with another Muslim from the North, Babagana Kingibe, became the first Nigerians that broke the barrier of ethnicity, religious sentiment, regional distrust and disunity in the nation. For the first time too, Nigerians voted without the problem of thuggery, murder and political bickering. Abiola had defeated his co-

contestant in the NRC even in his own hometown in the elections.

It seemed Nigeria was in the break of a new dawn, thanks to the political foresight of the man IBB. As Abiola coasted home to victory and the victory song was about being sung to usher Nigeria into another era after a long seemingly endless transition, the Northern feudal lords moved in swiftly. It seemed some of them suddenly realized that they were suddenly losing their God-given birthright to the South in an unexpected manner. If they must allow power to shift, they had to negotiate it. It had not been negotiated in the pre-June 12 era. This much they demonstrated as events unfolded.

The General moved quickly to halt the results of the election. The election was annulled and Nigeria was throne into chaos. Abiola won the election overwhelmingly such that people of all ethnic colorations had voted for him. He had achieved a feat that no Nigerian leader had ever achieved. He was the choice of the masses. His race, his tribe, his religion mattered less to Nigerians. He was the star that has deemed for Nigerians. He was the economic succor Nigerians wanted. He was the liberation that the masses sought. This victory was overwhelming and an intimidation of Northern pride. The problem was, Abiola was not 'born to rule'.

The annulment of the June 12, 1992 elections raised questions that had long been overdue. What were the bases of our co-existence if we were not equal citizens in the union? Why must leadership be the exclusive right of the North, which contributes little to the common purse that we share? Why must one region always be the antagonist in every situation making life unbearable for the others? Why could Southerners not live in peace in the North as the Northerners live in the South? Why must the producers of the resources that sustain the entire nation be the victims of political, religious, ethnic and development of infrastructure marginalization?

For the first time, Nigerians across the nation reacted violently. The nation seemed to be heading for another war. The nation was on the brink of collapse. General Babangida had lost control of the situation as Nigerians, in one voice, called for his resignation and the installation of the winner of the election. He was almost consumed by the game he had begun to play. The North did not expect the kind of resolve that followed the fight for the actualization of the June 12 election. General Babangida hurriedly and honorably bowed out foisting an interim contraption on Nigerians.

For the first time Nigerians, from the grassroots to the elites vehemently rejected the military and dared them. Babangida stepped aside without proffering any solution but creating a proper and conducive atmosphere for his long time associate in the business of coup making to take over the reins of government in the person of General Sanni Abacha. His coming was thought to be a solution to the deep mess that the gap-toothed General had plunged the nation. He thus termed his administration as a 'Child of Necessity'.

In the fight for the actualization of June 12, Nigerians erred, the major players erred, the advisers erred and too many wrong footings were carried. One of such was the court declaration of the Interim National Government illegal without the court ordering that the validity of June 12 election be restored. The second was in urging General Sanni Abacha to take over because of his perceived sentiment against the annulment of the election.

The fighters had thought he was coming to right the wrongs of June12 elections. They never knew that he was the very soiled finger behind the annulment. He was the very shadow behind the annulment. It was for him that his friend had been tinkering with the destiny of Nigeria. He was the much unseen hand of annulment. His coming to power was hailed as he met severally with the agitators for the actualization of June 12 who encouraged him to take over. He started by appointing some of them into his new cabinet. He was able to break the ranks of the proponents of June 12 actualization by successfully removing the Northern elements in the struggle.

Next he targeted some strong Yoruba and Ibo leaders, and made sure they participated in his government to give the impression he had come to right the wrongs of June 12. By the time he was done, the fight for June 12 had begun to look like a tribal war of the Yorubas against other tribes. General Abacha was a different thing entirely. Something that Nigerians would only imagine could happen in any other African country but not Nigeria. Abacha was a replication of the legendary Idi Amin of Uganda. He had come smoking, even in dark goggles ready to crush anything that stood in his way as opposition. His first victim was the all-powerful Sultan of Sokoto. The all-powerful Sultan was deposed and another imposed. He went in the guise of fighting corruption only to convert the nation's treasury to his family's bank account.

Oppositions were either eliminated or hauled into prison. Those who could escape went on exile but not before Chief M.K.O. Abiola had been arrested and hauled into prison. Anyone that dared his resolve was arrested and killed. The late General Musa Yar'Adua was a victim. One interesting thing however was that he had no tribal affiliation that Nigerians began to wonder if he were ever a Nigerian. He favoured no tribe above any other. He concentrated his effort at ruthlessly crushing all opposition on his way to becoming a civilian president. Minority agitation in the Niger-Delta began to gain fervor in his regime but he soon dealt decisively with that. He promptly executed the leaders of the crusade.

Abacha had no business with infrastructural development. That responsibility was given to the once self-righteous, self-styled disciplinarian, northern demi-god, self-acclaimed only savior of Nigeria and former Head of State, General Mohammadu Buhari who had demeaned his own stature to serve in the government of Abacha as chairman of Petroleum Trust Funds.

Abacha was busy lining his own pocket with national loot while Buhari was busy helping to further impoverish the South with his Petroleum Trust Fund (PTF). Abacha was preoccupied with his ambition of becoming civilian dictator while Buhari was busy using PTF to further the cause of North development. He was routing all opposition to even bother with the isolation of Nigeria from the international community. He had little patience with any one who dared his regime with riots and strikes. He meted the same punishment to Southerners, Northerners, Hausas, Yorubas, Ibos or minority. He held no friendship allegiance to anyone. What mattered to him most was his own interest and anyone who was against such perceived personal interest was an opponent to be eliminated.

His ambition to transit from military to civilian president was the utmost deal. Abacha held the entire nation to a stand still at gunpoint. The transition programme drawn by him was for him alone. No one was allowed to participate in it. He was the draftsman, the reviewer, and the author of the constitution. Those that would sing his praise were those allowed to be members of his five political parties. He was the de facto parties' chairman as well as the only presidential candidate of the five parties that his cronies had formed. He became a demigod to the nation and everyone had to pay abeyance to him in Abuja.

Abuja became a shrine where the people must go and worship the leader. He barely left his domain to see or mix with the people he governed. He was himself a prisoner of the same power that he sought so much. He dared anyone to challenge him to contest. He maintained a pretentious tough stance against corruption that actually was a deception at fooling Nigerians to look away from his avaricious attitude and that of his family. In less than five years, he had embezzled from Nigeria twice as much as what all the leaders that ever ruled Nigeria put together had embezzled.

Nigerians became sycophants for fear of being eliminated. They danced and sang to the tune he played. Other greedy ones sang his praise so that they could help themselves to part of the loot. Only those who played his card dined and wined with him from the pot of cookies in the treasury. Anyone who did not kow-tow his line found his way out of the country. Suppressed agitation had begun to build up despite his seeming non-tribal posture. One part of the nation was more on the receiving end of his draconian style while the other tagged along with him.

The South was brutally on the receiving end. The South could not stomach the deliberate trampling on their right. Agitation began for Sovereign National conference of ethnic nationalities. It was obvious that the nation would collapse on the dark goggled General. By then too many framed-up innocent bloods and supposedly guilty bloods had been shed by the General. Among his victims were the late Mrs. Kudirat Abiola, wife of the late Chief M. K. O. Abiola, winner of the annulled June 12 elections, Chief (Pa) Alfred Rewane, Rtd. Major General Shehu Musa Yar'Adua, Chief Olusegun Obasanjo (lucky to have survived his jail), Kenule Saro-Wiwa, and too many others. Others went on exile to escape the rage of his guns and brutal misrule.

The only way, to save the nation and preserved the territorial contraption called Nigeria was to murder the two players on the stage. General Sanni Abacha was murdered, and Nigerians rejoiced on the streets. No one was interested in how a man that who had hosted Yasar Arafat just the previous day died overnight in his sleep. Nigerians were too glad to have him out of the scene that no one asked questions. After all, his own hands had been stained with the blood of so many innocent Nigerians.

Till date, no one from official circles still in or out of government gave Nigerians any reasonable explanation as to why the elections of 1992 were annulled neither has anyone offered apologies for it. June 12 was not only annulled, Abacha's life was annulled. After he annulled the Interim National Government, he also annulled the lives of, Alhaja Kudirat Abiola, Pa Alfred Rewane, Ken Saro-Wiwa and lots of others.

If Nigerian were glad at the annulment of Abacha's life without apology, the decimators got it wrong with the annulment of Chief M. K. O. Abiola's life. He died mysteriously in the same manner that Abacha died. The Americans had to come and carry out a post-mortem, to ascertain that he was not actually murdered to douse the tension. The death of Abiola thus set the stage for a new direction after about seven years of tension that was almost leading to the collapse of the nation.

It was obvious that the step aside General had positioned himself for the new king maker role that he was to play in the post June 12 Nigeria. General Abdusalam Abubakar emerged the choice of the new regime obviously a choice from Minna. General Abubakar was not ready for leadership and obviously on Minna's advice had assumed leadership. His transition programme was all he gave Nigeria. The North had begun to shop for someone that must keep Nigeria in tact and preserve her interest. This resolve saw the General from Minna traveling to Otta after all political detainees were freed.

The reign of Abacha and IBB seems to have made a saint out draconian Buhari's regime. The anomaly and aberration called military rule that has supervised the squandering of a nation's legacy for several years has reached it crescendo and had no idea any more on how to move the nation forward. The only option left for the drivers of this dilapidated vehicle called Nigeria knew that they had to quit the center before things would fall apart.

By the time Abacha had finished with Nigeria, there was a great human waste as well as squandering of the nation's resources. Looting was unprecedented in the history of Nigeria by a man who claimed had been fighting corruption. Men of low intelligence wasted brilliant Nigerians. The North was on the path of reconciliation with the South and offered to lend power to the South. General Ibrahim Badamosi Babangida, the step aside leader of Nigeria, had become the nationalist saddled with the responsibility of keeping the nation in tact as one indivisible entity.

DEMOCRACY AS FOISTED ALTERNATIVE TO SOVEREIGN NATIONAL CONFERENCE (SNC)

The IBB and Abacha years witnessed the period in the life of this nation with the most clamour for SNC and Resource Control by ethnic militias and groups. Pro-Democracy groups emerged to fight the military rulers to a standstill demanding for the disengagement of the military from national politics,

IBB worked assiduously to see that this power lending worked well to the favour of the North. Power had to be negotiated with the South. The North thus went into negotiation with the South to lend power to it so that the nation can remain one. The general had to make several trips down South to discourse with the favoured choice of the North in the person of the former head of state, a retired General now Chief Olusegun Obasanjo.

Chief Olusegun Obasanjo was and is indeed the true child of destiny, having another date with history. He indeed had an appointment to keep with his destiny in the affairs of the nation. His Second Coming after a brief spell in the gulag of Abacha to say the least was divinely ordained. His was the anointed messiah that the North wanted to use to wield the nation together and continue the colonialisation of the South as passed on to them by the British.

Obasanjo had played the Northern script in his first coming and if the North had thought he was still the same person, his coming to power again proved that all wrong. Rejected by his own people at the polls, the man was undaunted as the North voted overwhelmingly for him in the 1999 elections. He won and set about cleanse the nation of the perceived injustice. His Second Coming showed age and maturity. He was now his own man and not anybody's stooge any more.

The regime of Olusegun Obasanjo who was forced on Nigerians by the ruling class or by the scheming of Retired General Ibrahim Badamosi Babangida and the then head of state, General Abdulsalami Abubakar was nothing but a dance of shame. The so-called generals insulted the patience of Nigerians by making them believe that he was the man for the job.

Corruption was taken to a new level under Obasanjo as the looting of the nation became unmatched since independence. Both at state and federal level, the politicians could not control their greed for money and the president's attempt at fighting corruption through the government organ, Economic and Financial Crime Commission (EFCC) was just another attempt at enriching himself.

Obasanjo refused to believe that there is an imbalance that needed correction in the system or that the nation needs a sovereign national conference or that the fight for resource control is justified. In his first four years in office, the same problem that had been the banc of unity within the nation had confronted him. Yet as a nationalist, he believes that time will correct the problems. These have been problems from the beginning. Right from 1914 and after almost a hundred years of amalgamation, the problems have refused to go away. The nation yet must continue in the groan of this injustice of a system that is fraught with fraud.

The soldier in him was wont to apply force in dealing with issues of national concerns. There was greater agitation for regional autonomy and resource

124

control under him, even the north began to agitate for the establishment of sharia law within their domain. Obasanjo's response was the use of brutal force to quell the agitations. Credit must be given to him for curtailing the agitations of his own people under the banners of Odua People's Congress and the massacre at Odi.

Through out his eight years tenure in the office, Obasanjo could not distinguish between military rule and democracy. He handled issues like a military man thus; Odua People's Congress, various Ijaw militant groups and Boko Haram movement in the north were dealt with military style to suppress their agitations. Likewise disfavored members of his cabinet as well as governors were harassed out of office while he and his sycophants looted the nation.

His was a politics of vendetta; he wanted to be seen as the messiah that rescued Nigeria from the brink of collapse. He had given so much to the nation without taking thus he became master of loot and corruption, amassing so much wealth for himself and his band of loyalists before planting another of his cronies Alhaji Musa Yar Adua in power when he exited from office.

The better part of Yar'adua's regime were spent in and out of the hospital before he eventually died in November 2009 paving the way for Dr. Goodluck Jonathan, the first southern minority to rule the nation. History beckoned on this man; it is his to fulfill or to waste. His administration spent the better part of its tenure battling religious insurgency and the Niger-Delta crisis. And while attempting to deal with the problems of Nigeria, corruption continued unabated and the nation plunged into further obscurity. Insecurity is still the order of the day. The politicians around him are clearly visionless and vague in their ideas and values for building a virile nation.

The administration of Goodluck Jonathan was an obvious disappointment. It is obvious that the problems of this nation were too great for the shoeless professor to handle. He was anything but convincing about his ability to handle the myriads of problems facing the nation. He too was overseeing an over bloated and corrupt executive that has been anything but caring about the situation in the nation.

Politicians seem to undermine his ability to run this country; he became the most disrespected politician and President in the history of this nation. In order to gain the respect of others, he overlooked in the corrupt attitude of the politicians that plundered the nation. Under him there was greater fight over oil and oil wealth and he used the greed of most Northern politicians for oil well to make them kow-tow his lines. He was almost a prisoner of the northern oligarchy as he did everything to please them to the displeasure of the rest of the country/

If there was anyone that had the chance to actualize the dreams of a better nation and the dreams of a true federation, that history fell on Jonathan who is from the region that has been at the forefront of this struggle. History beckoned on him to actualize the dream of his people by convoking a Sovereign National Conference where the future of this nation would be have been discussed and the basis of our national coexistence reexamined. However, the shoeless professor chose to squander the opportunity leaving the masses at the mercies of glutonic corrupt generation of leaders whose only concern is for their pockets and not the survival of the nation or the welfare of the masses.

When Jonathan chose to convene a national dialogue or conference as he called it, it was obvious that he too has begun to see democracy as an option to sovereign national conference just like his predecessors like Chief Olusegun Obasanjo. It is a pity that most politicians who were once agitators for resource control and sovereign national conference now believe that democracy is an option that has made the call for a sovereign national conference obsolete, some of them even participated in Jonathan's national dialogue.

And then he was thrown out of Aso Rock by the collusion of the northern powers that he had pleased in his six years as president of the nation as the dictator and agitator for northern dominance, an unrepentant religious bigot, who has a dream of Islamizing the nation, ascended the throne. For Buhari's performance, it is rather early to access but the first one year of his rule has seen increased activities of massive killings of other tribes by heavily armed Fulani jihadists marauding as herdsmen and slaughtering whole clans while President Buhari has ignored his people's excesses in the name of fighting corruption but would spare no gun in sending the entire nation army to Niger Delta to deal with militants for the reason of our so-called commonwealth – crude oil.

The honest question one should ask is have Nigerians really lived together like one people in almost one hundred years after the amalgamation? Have we been able to overlook our religious, ethnic, regional, state, community differences and then live together as one? These questions beg for answers, almost a hundred years of co-existence within the British constructed nation called Nigeria?

After independence, have the leaders been sincere to themselves in handling the problems putting aside their own tribal, ethnic and religious differences? The fact is that Nigerians are wont to pretend that these problems do not exist. The leaders are the biggest traitors of the people. They see the problem with the nation when they are outside the system and close their eyes to it and pretend we can live around it once in power.

The result had been that the masses have not been the better for it. They are the suffering lots. Leaders wear the toga of nationalism to defraud the people of their God-given rights and trample upon their future. These are anti-changes and would rather maintain the status quo to keep the people in perpetual slavery.

Everything is taken away from the people including their right to good life. Good life has become elusive while the looters bulge daily with the life drained from the people. Any attempts at protesting leads to the hangman's noose. The people live in constant fear of their rulers and awe of the system that has deprived them of their life. This is the lot of the Nigeria masses and worse for the people of Niger Delta masses.

Is democracy thus an option that has made sovereign national conference an unwarranted demand? Has democracy replace our need to reshape the course of our national history? Should we forget the call for a sovereign national conference because we are now in the era of democracy?

This democracy is too expensive; the people are paying for the excesses of our politicians while a wider gap is being created between the rich and the poor. The wealth of the Niger-Delta is enriching the others in the union while the region still suffers neglect and poverty.

Democracy is not an option for a sovereign national conference; the nation needs to talk at a sovereign level as determined by the people, not at the level set up by the politician. And the people should be allowed to choose their own reps not selected loyal party members so that this nation may survive.

A run down through our democratic experience shows that the solution to the problems of this nation does not lie in democratic experiments. The people are still under intense suffering. Corruption has continued unabated just like since independence. The politicians are confused on how to move the nation forward. The parties are extensions of each other with the same political brigades. We are moving in an endless circle. It is obvious that the problems of Nigeria are greater than Goodluck Jonathan, greater than a Buhari and an Atiku.

Indeed the problem of the nation is greater than all the politicians put together. We have to go down to the basics, only a movement from the grassroot can solve the problems of the country and this is the people coming together and determining that this nation and its configuration has to be rebuilt from its foundation. We have to put away tribal sentiments, religion has to be relegated to the background, the people's assembly has to be convened. The decision is a sovereign national conference to correct all the anomalies inherent in our forced amalgamation.

If we do not go back to the drawing board we will continue in the same endless circle of experimentation of nationhood that is bound to failure. We will salvage this nation only from the grassroot. The masses must force the hands of the leaders just like it did in the military era, we have to come to the people's assembly and negotiate the basis of our coexistence so that leaders would know their level of accountability, so that regions can glow in the economies of complementarities and not dependence on a decaying source.

CHAPTER EIGHT

THE DAMAGE OF MILITARY RULE ON THE PSYCHE OF THE SOCIETY

To say that the greatest crime on humanity outside slave trade was the scramble for African land by the Europeans through colonialism would be stating the obvious. But greater crime was perpetrated in Nigeria in the forceful amalgamation of the North and South in 1914 without consultation with the people. The granting of independence without extending the opinion that excised Cameroon from Nigeria, to the rest of the people, mostly the minorities, further worsened the crime.

The next crime on the nation was the Nzeogwu's coup that disrupted a normal process of national growth. That Ironsi accepted the responsibility of leading and arrogating power to himself against popular opinion was debasing the very essence of independence. That Gowon agreed to lead the butchering mission of the North against the South made him an enemy of the people and a driver in the class of modern despots. Murtala's role is commendable because the singular reason he came was to return power to the people.

That Buhari came on the scene to dehumanize the society further made him an accomplice in the fight against the sensibility of Nigerians. His overthrow by IBB, the man who gave Nigeria an aimless transition made the man IBB a slave driver in the class of the others. Abacha of course came to bury the coffin that had been nailed by his predecessors. This long chain of military over-lordship had begun to affect the psyche of both young and old Nigerians. It was becoming the vogue to militarize all the facet of the National life. Nigerians were becoming aggressively patient and dictatorial in all positions of authority.

Annulment especially under the IBB and the Abacha regimes had crept into every establishment. Nigerians in positions of authority were becoming maximum leader and the acronym 'NADECO' was labeled on all forms of opposition or resistance. Imposition of stooges and political sycophants that will sing leaders praise had become the culture in the society. This was the culture that IBB and Abacha gave to Nigerians that even the traditional institution lost its relevance in the nation.

Traditional institution became a parastatal of the military institution. The natural rulers must pay homage to the rulers to become palace jesters in the court of the maximum rulers. Crumbs from the tables of these transiting military rulers fall to the grassroots natural leaders who after their brief spell in Abuja still return to their domains to become again, subjects of their royal majesties.

The maximum rulers arrogated to themselves the duties of local king-makers in the selection processes of natural rulers for various communities. They tinkered with the tradition and culture of a people to which they were most time aliens. As a result of this, so many communities to this day remain in crisis. Leaders whose rights did not include the ruling their people have been imposed as rewards for their loyalty to the maximum leaders. This made most natural rulers lose the respect of their subjects which they had to fight hard to regain.

The larger society had become infested with corruption and lack of patriotism. Success became measured in monetary terms. Traditional rulers put up the titles in their kingdoms for sale to the highest bidders. It was a case of the better you are at stealing and looting of the nation's wealth to become rich the greater your respect amongst your kinsmen. Overnight millionaires were created without recourse to hard work. Hard work is no longer rewarded by the Nigerian society but mediocrity. The average Nigerian became easy wealth crazy and not hard work crazy as they turned to vices like yahoo-yahoo, 419, drug peddling, etc.

As a result, the nation polity was infested with cultists. Cultists ruled all the facets of life and had a field day on the civil service. The legal system was also infested as justices were often perverted. Justice became the preserve of those who could afford it. The police force till today has not wriggled itself out of the problem, as the law enforcers became crime enforcers. The police became the society's enemy as the corruption within it became unequalled and carried to the open. The society had to begin to form vigilante groups to secure their lives and property within their neighborhood, a sign that there was no law in the nation. The nation was indeed in need of redemption.

The academic institution was also worse for it. The nation's institutions were plagued with various strikes, as the tertiary institution had been left to decay for long. The universities were left in decay. There were no research facilities in the schools as billions of Naira was sunk in white elephant projects as a means to embezzle state funds. As at 1991, 1992, 1993-2001, most tertiary institutions could not boast of functional library with good books for research.

Academic pursuits in the country became reserved for the wretched of the society. Lecturers had become the least paid salary earners. The pursuits of educational goals were no longer based on excellence as most universities had gone commercial (PLC). Certificates were sold to the highest bidders. The lecturers became scores traders. Students who could pay the asking price were usually awarded the best marks. The ladies that could fulfill their lusts became the brightest.

The rot that the military rule brought into the society in the late 1980s and 1990s was unprecedented in the history of the nation. General Sanni Abacha even went ahead to appoint military sole administrators into some of the nation's tertiary institutions. The Ahmadu Bello University Zaria, University of Nigeria Nsukka are cases in point. In the Buhari era, the regime had threatened that any institution that dared it would be turned into military barracks. It was obvious that these leaders had no regards for academic pursuits. This threat was almost achieved by the Abacha government.

The universities became grounds for the pursuit of negative activities that were inimical to academic goals. The academic environment became an extension of the society. The Vice Chancellors became autocratic in their mode of running the institutions. They were collaborators with the military in the killing of the tertiary education. Institutions began to be run like private estates of the V.C's. Their problems became that of opposition to lean purse of the institutions.

The institutions due for want of proper academic pursuits became cult infested in the manner that the society had become so infested. The cults found patronage in the Vice Chancellors who were looking for alternative means of quelling the powers of the ever-militant students' union bodies. The Vice Chancellors began to use the students' cults and state machinery to dislodge vibrant students' union leaders. They annulled union elections at will where it did not suit their agenda.

Any lecturer who did not belong to the VCs group on any campus were termed NADECO and framed up in the Abacha era. The VCs could not condone oppositions from the students' union or from the Academic Staff Union of Universities (ASUU). These two groups had to be dislodged from the campuses. Examples were the universities of Lagos, Benin, Ilorin, etc where cult activities assumed gruesome dimension. This was as a result of the encouragement they got from the school authorities in their bid to get rid of the students' union. Any students' union leader not playing to the script of these schools authorities was labeled cult member and expelled especially in the periods between 1991, 1992-2000.

The autocratic VCs who invaded these institutions within these periods aided the total militarization of the academic institutions. The academic institutions had always been the bedrock of any revolutionary thoughts in the developmental stage of any nation. No revolutionary ideas succeed without the active participation of the students' population. The Vice Chancellors who had been produces of the most comfortable learning environment helped the military to reduce the education system to a mere shadow of what they had passed through. They helped to make national investment in manpower development a commercial venture.

It was unfortunate that while discouraging unionism, the best tool against the military elite then, the institutions were breeding an alternative to it – the rise of cultism. Students that were supposed to be cohesive in their fight against the oppressive tendencies of some authorities became tools in the head of the very authority from which they sought to protect themselves. The cultists rose to take over the role of the union leaders. They were supported by the whims of the school authority itching to impress the military rulers who had issued warnings to them to keep their domain keys and locks.

A microcosm of the Nigeria situation was built within the academic institutions. Like the nation, tribal, cultic, and personal interest became the order within the institutions. Terror was unleashed and lives lost. Before the nation knew it, its reality had gone beyond control. The academic institutions had become grounds for breeding vicious citizens who come into the society as high tech hired killers and sophisticated robbers in the highest class rather than ground for academic pursuit and talent development.

Students' union leaders became the victims of this new wave of assault both within the campuses and the civil society. Union leaders lost their lives, some expelled and unionism became an extension of school administration as students' union leaders became school prefects. The campuses became military barracks as military tanks and soldiers were permanently stationed by the gates. By 1998, genuine unionism was completely dead and cultism had risen to its highest crest. The cultists had taken over the office of the union leaders with the connivance of the school authority.

At the same period, the nation had lost some of its finest academics to the brain drain. They had been employed by other nations that value their services more than their fatherland. This was the nation of our dream, a nation chained by its own leaders. The nation was indeed sick.

On the society, the Nigerian had become so poor in the midst of so much wealth. This oil wealth has impoverished the Nigerian and enriched the leaders. In every facets of life the vast majority of over 90% of Nigerians are confronted with hunger, starvation. He lives in abject poverty in homes unfit for even the swine of the imperialists. Poverty, crimes and youth unemployment had become hydra-headed problems of a nation exporting over two million barrels of crude oil per day.

Basic amenity to provide the minimal comfort for Nigerians was non-existent. Yet, under these conditions leaders stashed away billions of the nation's loots in foreign land. The Nigerian came to accept his fate. It is a fact that the average Nigerian on the street did not trust the leaders and believed everyone was just like the other. To the average Nigerian, if the nation's wealth must be share monetarily, he preferred the little change that will get to him because he had lost fate in the nation.

He has come to accept poverty as his lot believing that one day he too can be made leader and then he could help himself with the nation's treasury. Thus there was nothing like national service or patriotic service, or pride of national service, his service must be measured in monetary terms. He attached this to his terms because his fatherlands would not come to his aid as an individual in his periods of needs. He believed in grabbing all he could for now, while the future takes care of itself.

The Nigerian does not see himself as a Nigerian first of all. He sees himself first in all things, as the leaders seem to have taught him to do. Then he sees himself as a native of somewhere where no other Nigerian can freely be part of without opposing the right of that Nigeria to freely choose the community. The nation is not his concern. He is only there to help himself to better his own lots not the lot of the others. And God helping if he had his way, every other Nigerian must be enslaved until he has helped himself to his satisfaction. This is the psyche of the typical Nigerian.

The military leaders who had wasted and plundered the nation do not feel any sense of responsibility towards the nation. For them, enough of the nation's wealth had been amassed for their unborn generations that the rest of the country could drift to collapse. The youths of the nation had been so wasted by the leaders that it is as if the nation is in hopeless drift. Tomorrow is as unsure as if yesterday never existed for the Nigerian. In all, it is the future of the youth that the leaders must mortgage to feed their own gluttonous ego.

On the part of the nation's treasury, it had been looting unlimited. Several billions of dollars in oil money belonging to the nation had been looted and never accounted for by various military regimes. The nation has been made poorer while Nigeria has produced some of the richest generals in the world. The other part of the economy has long been neglected that they have become almost irredeemable. Every farmer has become oil magnate, every cattleman has become oil license holder, and every trader on the street has become oil sheikh while the Niger Delta groans under neglect.

The military institution has indeed done so much damage to the Nigerian and perpetrated the falsehood upon which the nation was founded. This few civilian administrations have not been bold enough to cry out against this perceived injustice except perhaps, for the late Prof. Ambrose Ali and the new generation of Southern leaders who had finally come to terms with the realities. The psyche of the Nigerian had been so damaged, the nation so damaged, the nationalities so damaged that no one believes in it any more.

One of greatest damage of military rule to the psyche of the average Nigerian is the mentality that there are three ethnic groups that matter the most in this union called Nigeria, that this nation is built on the foundation of the three major tribes of Nigeria namely; Hausa/Fulani, Yoruba and Igbos. This shows that there is no regard for the minority tribes in nation.

This campaign was given prominence under the IBB and Abacha administration, a currency denomination N50 (fifty naira note) nicknamed WAZOBIA – a coinage from the three languages of Hausa, Yoruba and Ibo, was created to promote this anomaly and distortions. This is to make every other tribe in the nation think only as a Yorubaman, Hausaman or as an Iboman. The impression right now is that the other ethnic groups have been submerged within these three groups so in Nigeria, we can only talk about the Yorubas, the Hausas and the Ibos.

The worst of all the damages of the incursions of the military into leadership process of the nation on the psyche of the average Nigerian is the notion of born-to-rule. The fact that a particular section of the country produced most of the military rulers in Nigeria gave the rest the impression that they were a conquered territory of the ruling feudal military lords.

It got so bad that the slogan of born-to-rule became the state motto of a particular state in the northern part of Nigeria. The other part of Nigeria felt like slaves in the nation that all were supposed to have the same stake in. In all the north has dominated leadership for thirty nine years of our over fifty four years of coexistence as an independent nation.

PART THREE

QUESTIONING THE BASIS OF GENERAL COEXISTENCE BY THE NATION'S ETHNIC NATIONALITIES

- **RESOURCE CONTROL**

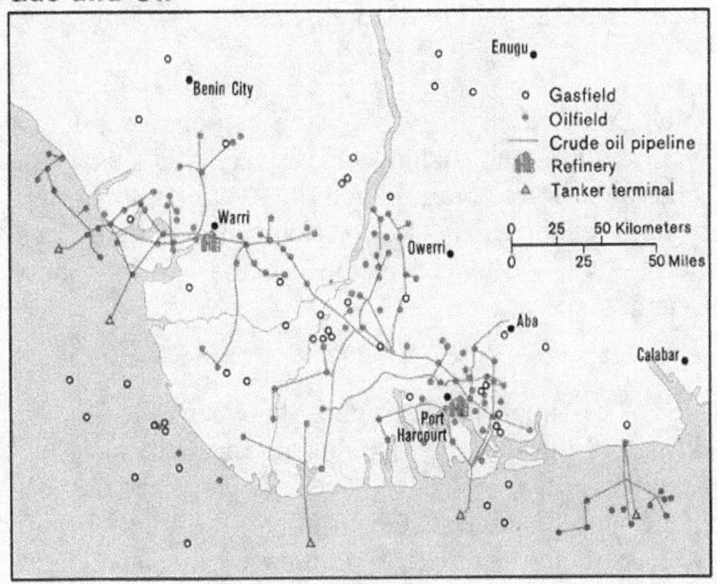

THE NIGER DELTA AREA

The Niger Delta area is located in the South-South geo-political zone of Nigeria.

AREA: 70,000 sq. km

ECOLOGICAL ZONES: Sandy   ridge   barriers, brackish or saline mangroves, fresh water permanent and seasonal swamp forests and lowland rain forests.

POPULATION: 14,000,000 people (EST.)

ETHNIC CONFIGURATION: Ijaw, Urhobo, Ibiobio-Anangs, Itshekiri, Ikwere, Ogonis etc. There are about 1,600 communities within the area.

ECONOMY: The mainstays of the region's economy were agriculture and fishing. However, this has been replaced by oil exploration activities, which over the years has rendered the once rich environment less productive and destroyed some of the world's best ecosystem.

CRISIS: The inter-ethnic fights between the Ijaws, Itshekiris and the Urhobos has become a national issue. These crises seem to have been fanned by the oil companies and the Federal Government. It initially began in 1952, with the vindictive politics of the late Chief Obafemi Awolowo and aided by the Military under General Sanni Abacha in the politics of LGA creation.

144

CHAPTER NINE

<u>QUESTIONING THE BASIS OF OUR CO-EXISTENCE</u>

From the beginning, the question of minority fears have been so pertinent that even the colonial authorities afraid that this might become an escalated problem in an independent Nigeria set up the Willink Commission. It was the minority question that first brought the question of the coexistence of the nationalities within the nation to the fore. This became a nagging question long after the colonialists had gone. This question became the concern of everyone in the South when the North went on rampage to massacre people of Southern origin especially the Igbos.

Prior to the civil war, the North had begun to dominate the nation political life while the West had dominated the economy. The coup of 1966 had also produced a counter coup led solely by Northern officers. This led to the slaughter of officers of Southern origin, in retaliation of what the North perceived as a coup against only the North. The massacre of Southerners in the North also led the East to reconsider the basis of its coexistence in the nation that offered little protection and prospect to its nationals.

The question of the basis of coexistence among the ethnic nationalities reared its head again in the coup led by the late Major Gideon Orkar. In his address to the nation, Major Orkar had announced that certain part of the country ceased to be part of the country until they successfully negotiate their readmission to the federation. It was the first time military officers openly displayed their anger at the mistake of amalgamation.

However, what the planners of the 1990 coup did not realize was that when such ideas are hatched, one does not just rely on the might of military fiat to achieve it. At that point, the people were not aware of the motive of the coupists who had themselves begun to fall apart as the then head of state, quickly turned their gains around. It was or would have been beautiful for the nation to negotiate the bases of her coexistence for which the average man had become weary.

The fact however, is that it was not just the core North that needed to negotiate with the rest of the country. The entire nation needed such negotiations. The Yorubas must negotiate, the Igbos must negotiate, and the Urhobos, the Itshekiris, Biroms, Jukuns, Igalas, Nupes, and so many others must negotiate. The negotiations should not have been limited to the core north alone. If we must continue to live together, we should understand why we must. We must spell out politically how the nation should be controlled so that everyone will have a sense of belonging. We should spell these out, so that life can be secure for anyone in wherever he chooses to reside and make home.

The third attempt was after the annulment of the June 12, 1993 elections. Then, the agitation had assumed a frightening dimension, as all ethnic nationalities from the South were vehement and unanimous in their call for a sovereign national conference. The Abacha era of waste, both in terms of resources and human lives, was the peak of such cries, as everyone had lost confidence in the federation.

146

Another question that has been of equal prominence has been the issues of resource control. Prior to the Saro-Wiwa tragedy, the first uprising against the system for the people to actualize themselves and control their resources was led by Isaac Adaka Boro. Isaac Adaka Boro was and still is the symbol of the Ijaw uprising today. What he believed in and died for, in the late 1960s is today the bane of the Nigeria nation. Isaac Adaka Boro was the first martyr of agitation for resource control in contemporary Nigeria. The political basis for the nation's coexistence had been hinged on this and this had begun to gain momentum by the new set of gladiators from the South who had come to realize the injustice inherent in the system.

As it appears, the powers that be are scared of the mention of the word resource control or the sovereign national conference, proffering that the issue has been taken care of with the nation's return to democracy. Those terms they say, portends danger for the nation's unity if allowed. The question is, if they are so convinced that there is justice in the present arrangement why are they afraid that the nation would break up if the issue was brought up. If they are so confident that the average Nigeria is happy with the present arrangement, then they should try the resolve of the Nigerian and see how much he believes in the indivisibility of the nation.

In the last hundred years as it would seem, the North had continued to dominate and drain the resources of the nation. They have depended on the South for self-sustenance. The belief it would seem is that there would be uneven development in the nation if the issue of resource control is allowed. The North would lag far behind in the scheme of development if the regions or states were allowed to control their resources. The present unitary-federalism is greatly in the favour of the North and every constitution and regime had maintained the status quo to favour the North.

But the question to ask is has almost a hundred years of pumping the South's resources into the North translated to a better life for the masses of the region? The answer obviously is 'NO', it has not. The average Northerner is still ravaged by poverty, illiteracy, diseases and hunger. This is because such wealth being looted is used to enrich the pockets of the elite who use religion to keep the people under the perpetual slavery of feudalism.

The Northern populace convinced that they have not had a fair share of the nation's wealth voted against their own when they voted for Abiola in the June 12 elections. It was the dangerous realization by the Northern oligarchy that they have been rejected in the polls that led the nation to a brink of collapse. The enlightened average Northerner even began to question the impact of the continued dominance of the nation's politics by its own people, on the teeming population of the North.

The agitation grew strongly in the South. The Yorubas questioned the basis of their coexistence in the nation, and so did the Ibos, the Ogonis, the Ijaws, and all the other groups. The North realizing the danger and confronted the damage that had been done to it's own agrarian economy through over reliance on the South swung into action to fish for a stabilizing factor from the South. That was the Second Coming of Chief Olusegun Obasanjo, this time as a civilian president.

His regime, massively elected in the North, was thus thought to have Southern body and a Northern soul by the average Nigerian of Southern extraction. On

148

assumption of office, Obasanjo began to show that he had grown twenty years different from the young man that bestrode the nation as a military head of state in 1976-1979. He began to show that he was a man with a national soul and not regional soul though with a little more tilt for his kinsmen over and above others.

The Northern masses are a curious lot, they would go with the aspiration of their leaders without minding how corrupt that leader is, they would kow-tow any line that gives them religious advantage over the south or the other Christian states. To the average northerner, a northern leader always signifies the dominance of the north over the south, of the Muslim over the Christian or the Hausa/Fulani over the rest of the nation. Thus when the masses were told by the consensus of northern leaders that Obasanjo was the choice, they all went out to vote for Obasanjo, this pattern showed again in electing Yardua, and showed in bringing Buhari back to power.

CHAPTER TEN

<u>ISSUES IN RESOURCE CONTROL</u>

Resource control cannot be discussed extensively without understanding the basic framework upon which the traditional Nigerian society was founded. This will illuminate some of the facts responsible for our audacious trudge towards nationhood. Any system founded on fraud and injustice experiences continuous agitation from the component units. Nigeria is a system made up of units. Each unit is supposed to perform various functions that ameliorate pressures from any one part. The human body is the exact example of this.

The brain thinks for the body, the eyes see for the body, the hands perform tasks for the body. The legs move the body around, the stomach is the energy factory for the body. The stomach cannot think for the body, when that happens, the entire body is in trouble. This is how components and units work without relying too much on one another to perform its task, but all the units are components of one body.

Before the official partitioning of the African territory amongst the Europeans, the British government had granted exclusive trade charter to the Royal Niger Company to trade on her behalf exclusively in the Niger area. The trade was mainly in agricultural produces and raw material produced within the Southern and the Northern part. The ethnic nationalities then had independent jurisdiction of deciding how they traded with the Europeans, they determine terms of trade on their own.

Natives pay taxes to their native authorities in the forms of community rents and other levies. The communities did not also determine the way an individual uses his plot of land or sells his produce so long as he met the communal obligations expected of him. Resources of each political entity were exclusive preserves of the community and such communities only pay royalty or tribute to the larger kingdom or community that had the sovereignty over it for protection.

What then are resources? This is a relative term, depending on the individual, the collective, time, circumstance, needs, technology and means. Resources are thus material items useful to the developmental needs of a collective or an individual. These developmental needs defer from community to community and from time to time. Thus what became resources to the Europeans were at that time, not useful to the African. An example is the rubber found growing wildly in the Benin kingdom which the Europeans desired but the Benin's had no use for.

These resources are either exhaustible or inexhaustible. Where the hand of man has developed it, they become inexhaustible as man can easily replace it through the same process used to make it. On the other hand when the factors controlling their availability are beyond man, meaning that such resources occur in nature, then they are exhaustible as these factors had taken thousands of years and sometimes millions of years to accumulate the resources on the earth. The latter groups of resources have been more controversial, playing significant roles in the politics of man as every race, every tribe, and every ethnic nationality has played the politics of who controls what and at what quantity.

Certain humans have been endowed with nature's blessing as by divine design or by divine providence. They have been abundantly endowed with so much of these natural resources. While on the other hand, some other races of people have found themselves in environments that bestow little to nothing on them save harsh environmental conditions. Some have been both lucky and unlucky to have both, harsh environment and abundant resources.

The desire to build empires over other tribes and control their political lives had often been driven by the urge to control the people's economic life. Thus so many wars fought by man had been economic war. In Africa, there were fights to open trade routes, fight to control markets, fights to collect tributes from other tribes etc. In pre-colonial Nigeria where the land tenure system held sway, families on behalf of the community controlled the land. The land is shared in accordance with the family needs.

The individual who farms the land pays tribute to the owning family or the community, which is commensurate to the harvest he makes on the land. In other areas where the individual holds the title to his land, the resources, in terms of harvest from such land belongs exclusively to him. Produces are exchanged in the market either at prevailing price or at his discretion.

At the advent of the Europeans into the area known as Nigeria today, a lot of produces, which hitherto had no basic use became useful in Europe and became the basic agricultural resources of the areas. Each of the nationalities was traded with basically as independent

152

entities as the Europeans recognized the sovereignty of the nationalities. The trade in various produces created new wave noveau riche natives that dealt on behalf of the Europeans with the locals.

After the partitioning of Africa, the charter granted the Royal Niger Company was revoked as the British government became the direct controller of the peoples' wealth. The volumes of trade increased as the colonial authorities bought directly from the people, levied them taxes and set up structures for their government. Produces like rubber, timber, palm oil, kola nut, cocoa, groundnut etc became prominent and big earners. With these produces came the growth of certain towns.

Sapele grew in prominence because of timber, Enugu grew because of coal, and Kano for groundnut, cocoa brought prominence to the West, as oil palm brought prominence to the East and the Mid-West. The nation almost became self sufficient in the production of both food and cash crops till the late 1960s. At the granting of self-rule to the regions in the early 1950s, the regions gained control of their regional economy. Awolowo controlled the cocoa trades, Ahmadu Bello controlled the groundnut trade, Nnamdi Azikiwe controlled the oil palm trade of the East.

The level of achievements of these trios within their regions is still the basis of comparison for modern day state governors. Programmes and infrastructural developments were in accordance with available resources generated by individual governments within their regions. Thus Chief Awolowo had excelled above all because outside cocoa, he had revenues from timber, rubber and palm oil too, as the old Mid-West was part of the Western region.

His records were unequalled, as he was able to establish the first African television station at Ibadan, the Western Nigeria Television (WNTV) now taken over by the Nigeria Television Authority. His free education programme placed the Western Region way ahead of other regions in educational development. He also established the Ikeja industrial estate to take care of industrializations.

He built the popular cocoa house in Ibadan and the O'dua Investment to trade and generate money for the government. He established the Sketch as the official government newspaper as well as a world class university at Ile-Ife. His roads construction programme is today still unsurpassed. The foresight of the late social welfarist was unequalled among his pairs. Awolowo's foresight had liberated the minds of the Westerners from any form of feudal lordship, giving them total independence in the affairs of the region.

There were no quotas on educational placements. There was no national restriction on employment as the regional governments controlled their labor. Things were done based on merit not on one's tribe or religion. The colonialist served as the stabilizing factor for the regions. The society handed over to the founding fathers was orderly. The crises that later destabilized the nation was expected as the founding fathers showed lack of foresight. They showed too early in the day that they were actually not ready for the responsibility of leadership. Ironsi met a system whose functionality he did not fully come to grasp with. He chose to run leadership the way the military organization is run and arrogated absolute powers to himself at the centre.

As the regions relished the control they had over agricultural produces, the same could not be said of mined minerals. The colonial administration through the 1946 mineral act appropriated all the minerals to itself. Thus minerals like coal, tin, gold, and columbite belonged exclusively to the colonial authority. This trend continued in the Gowon's land use act and the petroleum act. Today, towns like Jos and Enugu are shadows of what they were in the days of colonialism.

Ironsi adopted the unitary system of government within four months of his coming to power. When Gowon came on the scene it was on the excuse that there was too much power at the centre. The nation's source of wealth changed as unprecedented earnings came from crude oil. As the system of government changed, so was the control of the regions over their resources. The federal government became the sole owner of resources and decided who gets what and the criteria of getting what was set by it.

The fraud became enormous as such ridiculous criteria as land mass, population and needs was among the criteria set by the federal government. In later times the federal government in its development plans began to toy with the idea of slowing the pace of developments in some areas so that other areas can catch up. Such was the retrogressive thinking of the government of the day. By that arrangement then, the states perceived as the most developed will get the least from federal purse while the least developed would get more.

As oil came, Niger-Delta, the producer of the oil wealth bled to develop the nation as it was kept constantly undeveloped despite its huge resources. As the new imperialist oil companies ably aided by the federal government plundered the Niger-Delta, the masses in the nation got worse off. The wealth found its way into private accounts in foreign lands. The oil companies aided by the leaders to impoverish the people declare false profits, false oil exploration figures and repatriated huge profits to develop their homelands. Money from this area was used to build other cities as Awolowo declared the place uninhabitable and not worthy of development.

The Niger Delta area became exposed to high level of environmental degradation. The farmlands were destroyed. The waterways polluted. The people were left with no means of livelihood as they were considered not educated enough to even work in these oil companies. Strangers came and discriminated against them in their own homeland in matters of employment. As the rest of the nation got richer, the Niger Delta got poorer. The oil wells were controlled from Lagos, which has the same physical terrain with the Niger Delta.

As the controllers or the local colonialists became weary of Lagos, they moved to Abuja, which today controls the oil wealth while the Niger Delta bleeds. The people of the Niger Delta had to sacrifice their lives and livelihood so that the rest of the other tribes of the nation can live and survive. Not even the crumbs were good enough for the people of the area. They got burnt up in crude fire, lost their farmlands to petrol fire, lost their fishing water ways to waste from crude pipes, live with carbon released into their atmosphere from flared gasses. In all these, the imperial oil companies and the government promoted disunity among the people and controlled the politics of the area so that the plunder can go on unabated had deliberately controlled the politics of the area.

The agitation for resource control by the states today is rightly justified. For one, the resource in the area is a non-renewable, injurious to the people and destructible to their land. The oil in Oloibiri has run dry and so are some other oil wells. In most of these communities, life has become worse than before oil were found on the land. The area has a unique problem and only the resources from the area can take care of it.

Pretending to recognize the peculiar needs of the environment and in other to pay special attention to the area, the first interventionist programme in post-independent Nigeria, the Niger Delta Development Board was set up by the Tafawa Balewa administration in 1962. Others had come after this, which in all cases had not been able to address this peculiar need of the people. They had been more of programmes meant to further dehumanize the people and their area as crude oil leprous infected area needing special care. The place has become worse off than the rest of the country.

Between 1962 and 1995, the area had become so impoverished that the average per capita income in the Niger Delta was less than the national average for the rest of the country. Yet the Niger Delta over the same period had contributed more than 90% of national earning to the federal purse.

Education, provision of basic health services, roads, and industries and in all other spheres of national development, the Niger Delta lagged behind the nation. The environment runs short of the minimum healthy environment required for human habitation. Oil spillage wreck untold harms on the people. Their agricultural lands are destroyed. Waterways have become toxic dumpsites, as fishing communities are rendered jobless. The people are bombarded daily with polluted air from gas flaring.

In one case of gas flaring in Sapele, Shell flared 944 million cubic meters of gas. According to International Institute for Democracy and Electoral Assistance, Nigeria in 1991 exceeded the international average for gas flaring by 72%. In that year, the world average was 4% of total production. In N.N.P.C.'s own records, approximately 2,300 cubic meters of oil are spilled in 300 different incidents yearly. Between 1976 and 1996, according to DPR (Department of Petroleum Resources), 4,835 incidents led to the spilling of 2,446,322 barrels, in which, 1,896,930 barrels were lost to the environment all within the Niger Delta.

These incidents began to breed an army of hostile youths whose land and environment has become harsh to him. He has to struggle for daily survival within an environment that provides wealth for other parts of the nation but cannot provide any means of livelihood for him. Worse still is the fact that, this wealth is flaunted before his very eyes. He goes out to see what transformation this wealth has brought on other regions yet the same wealth has been like a curse to his own community.

Is the fight for resource control by ethnic nationalities not a justified one considering the long period of neglect by those that had been in charge before now of the homeland? The question of course first and foremost is what constitutes resource control? Is it just increasing the constitutional provision of 13% to about

50%, 60% or even 70% and then leave it like that as some people have proposed?

No, resource control entails more; it is the participation of every level of government, from the grassroots to the federal government, in the exploration and management- utilization of proceed of the resource from such community. Thus the federal government, the state government, the local government and the community are all involved in the process of utilization, management and the politics of control of their resources. This means that each community is the custodian of its own resources first and foremost before all the other levels. Thus the community tailors its own developmental needs towards its peculiarity with the state government acting as the umpire. The community runs own budget based on the present and future needs of such community and the amount of revenue accruing to it from oil or other economic activity proceeds.

The States government acts as balancing force for areas within the states, whose resources do not meet their needs, while the federal government plays the same role for the states within the federation. This is the true basis for equity. Resource control transcends just the control for the crude oil deposits within the Niger Delta but also all other resources be they agricultural, natural or artificial resources within the environment. This is a fight that all Nigerians must embrace. It is also a fight for the individual to be able to actualize himself within a society that gives no room for self-actualization but leaves room only for recycling of leaders.

In this struggle, the people of Niger Delta must thus have a definite focus on what they want? What they are fighting for? To this end the people and leaders must be steadfast to present a united and cohesive front, which had been the bane of the Niger Delta. They must recognize that as neighbors living within the same environment from years of cordial relationship, though the politics of the Nigeria nation has corrupted to defraud the people, they are not the enemies within themselves.

The enemy is the oppressive system that takes away the right of the people to their land, and resources. The system that promotes mediocrity at the expense of excellence is the enemy. The system that takes away the people's means of livelihood to build a future for the children of mediocre who by means of state fiat were opportune to rule with the blood of the nation. The enemy is the system that delegates one tribe as inferior to the other and thereby promotes tribalism, nepotism, as means of national cohesion. The common enemy of the people is the system that takes away the opportunity of everyone to develop his potentials without placing inhibiting factors.

It is the system that keeps the people in perpetual slavery while plundering their resources. It is the very oppressive tendency that sought to quench the agitation for a people's inalienable right. The common enemy is the system that decides the people's destiny for them without their consent. It is the system that takes away a people's right to self-actualization. It is the system that the people must work hard to change. This system transcends class, religion, tribe and political leaning or ideology.

It behooves the masses to rise up against it, no matter one's religion, tribe, tongue, political association and social status. Resource control, true federalism is a must for Nigeria and the only peaceful means is a Sovereign National Conference. The people must sit

160

down and truly say 'We the Nationalities and peoples of Nigeria…have thus so and so resolve to live together under so and so conditions'. The people must also decide on what factors bind or dissolves them from the union and what compensation results from the violation of such agreement.

The system so built will recognize the fact that any system is made up of smaller units and accord the recognition first and foremost to the units. This is a collective fight. The fears of the pessimists that it would cripple the union or contraption called Nigeria are unfounded. It is the system that is a bit crippled to reduce the high tech corruption and attraction to it. Thus anyone serving there becomes nationally committed and not *pocketfully-committed*.

IMPLICATIONS OF RESOURCE CONTROL

Resource control from the foregoing simply put is the control and management of the resources in a locality from within the locality. This means the authority of the nationalities become the building blocks of the nation. The leaning pillar is the central government. The pillar will become useless without mutual respects amongst the building blocks. The question is will the foundation holding the building knit very well together if this is allowed? Will security and national unity become weakened? No, so long as the importance of every block is emphasized and each respects the other knowing that each plays a very important role in the building of the nation. And so long as the centre recognizes that its

161

beauty comes from the units and that beauty should be maintained and jealously guarded.

The protagonists of resource control argue that resource control is divisive. The truth is that, the present system has brought more distrust and suspicion among the ethnic nationalities than resource control could ever have. The feeling of being cheated creates more distrust. Justice and equity brings trust. This is what resource control brings. It will reawaken the people to their collective destiny. In less developed states with less potential, development of basic amenities and agricultural infrastructure will be pursued vigorously. They will develop a tax system that places so much responsibility on the leaders who will not be morally justified to tax a people they do not provide for. The present system is defrauded even by Nigerians who evade tax payment because they have no sense of duty to the leaders who themselves cannot ask for it.

The burden on the Federal government reduces as the other levels are saddled with greater responsibilities. The regions/states would do everything to keep their states safe for investment opportunities. The federal government then can direct investors based on their area of business interest to regions most investor friendly to such investment. That means that the states specialize in areas of comparative advantage based on the resources they can muster within their domain. The centre is alive to the protection of its citizens as holding factor making sure that the agreements between the ethnic nationalities are respected and kept by all.

With this, the people become one and they grow faster to become Nigerians than what presently obtains. Everyone identifies with the nation more as they feel safe, not scared that anyone will molest them or challenge them if they so chose to build their homes in any part of the nation. They also become free to change ethnic identity at will if they so will. Thus one can come from Sokoto and become a Deltan or from Maiduguri and become a Lagosian living freely among the people and like the people, not having to form another ethnic colony within the people.

National security becomes everyone's one fight and no particular ethnic group or religion or individual will have the monopoly of violence. Since the nationalities have agreed to live together under the specified condition and not constitution, the terms are strictly respected by all. Then Nigerians will begin to live with each other as coequals in the advancement of the nation. Then Nigerians can be truly patriotic. Services to the nation can become more selfless and not influenced by monetary gains. After all who will serve a nation that gives no respect to patriotism, whose leaders display astounding personal wealth and citizen are so poor.

Resource control and true federalism does not threaten national security and peace of the nation but enhances it. Regional autonomy gives more security. Slavery, which the present system represents, has never given a people the desired peace and security in the history of mankind. The Egyptians had no peace for as long as the Israelites were under them. The Ethiopians had no peace until Eritrea was excised from it. Israel has not known peace for appropriating portions of Palestinian land. Morocco's attempt at annexing Spanish Sahara has not been successful. The Hutus and Tutsis laid Burundi to waste before they became united through agreement to stop the slavery of one over the other. Sudan was the hot bed of revolution against a Northern slavery over the

South. Only a recent referendum freed the South from Northern domination of Southern resources.

Czechoslovakia is history because the various ethnic groups were lumped together by the communists without the people's consenting agreement. Yugoslavia is no more on world map for the same reason. In Spain the government has been fighting decades of ethnic insurrection. In India, Pakistan went their way due to irreconcilable differences at independence. It is more dangerous to suppress the will of the people than to allow them freedom for self-actualization.

CHAPTER ELEVEN

THE FRAUDS

The frauds on the Niger Delta begun at the advent of the British and had been greater since the colonialists granted self-rule to Nigerians. The plunder of the area had continued both by the Europeans, the Americans and the federal government. All had been in the battle for the soul of Niger Delta as well as the Niger Deltans. While the formers had fought to keep their imperialist hold on the area, the latter had fought against the continuous plunder of the area.

Within the federation, the Niger Delta occupies the area known as the South-South geo-political zone. The zone is divided into six states with one hundred and twenty three local government areas. Nigeria is a federal republic with thirty-six local government areas. In the North, Kano and Yobe states put together have sixty-five states. The entire region in which these two states belong have all together has one hundred and eighty local government areas. The entire nation has a total of seven hundred and sixty-nine local government areas with the North accounting for four hundred and forty four.

The implications of this is that the Niger Delta producing more than eighty percent (>80%) of the nation's income has just one hundred and twenty three parts or 15.995% of the share accruing to the local governments from the federation accounts, whereas, the North-West, contributing less than three percent (3%) to same account, has one hundred and eighty parts or

23.41% of same. So where is the justice in the system? It is even more pathetic to note that the said amount shared among the local governments is most times less than 25% of the total money shared between the states, the LG's and the federal government.

Next is the collaboration of the oil prospecting companies who are the partners of the Europeans in neo-colonialism and modern slavery? These chief collaborators are Shell, Chevron, Mobil, etc. The greatest injustice is perpetrated within this geopolitical zone whose environmental and human resources have been so abused and wasted in the name oil prospecting. The race for the soul of the area is that of robbers in a hurry to cart away the wealth of its victims. It is as if these companies are in hurry to dig every available land in the area and leave the place to waste. They are like thieves in a race against time.

Crude oil in the Niger Delta area is mined in an area covering about 75,000 square kilometers of sedimentary basin fill. The area contains about 20 billion barrels of oil, which the oil companies deplete at the rate of 15%. This is official figure, no account is given of the oil that these companies defraud the country and the Niger Delta through the activities of white bunkerers who come to their offshore locations to load illegal crude. Presently, production is between 2.5 million and 3.3 million barrels per day, depending on OPEC's quota. These were early 2000 estimates, the government expected that from the year 2010, the country would produce or the Niger Delta would cough out 4 million barrels per day to feed on the nation's lust. The natural gas deposit within the area is estimated at 120 trillion cubic feet.

About 5,284 wells have been drilled mostly in the Niger Delta. Presently, the Niger Delta has about 606 oil fields (increasing daily) from which oil flow. 355 of these are onshore while the remaining 251 are offshore. In Nigeria today, Shell, Chevron, Mobil, Agip, and Texaco control 98% of crude activities. Shell controls about 45% of total operation while the remaining 55% is left to the other companies in the area.

With the petroleum act, the federal government is the owner of all the oil wells in the country and controls, its management and exploitation through NNPC which in turn goes into joint venture agreement with these companies to deploy their capital to the area to prospect for oil. Below is the share of the equity of the federal government in the joint venture schemes.

Shell	NNPC 55% Shell 30% Agip5% Elf 10%
Mobil	NNPC 60% Mobil 40%
Chevron	NNPC 60% Chevron 40%
Agip	NNPC 60% Agip 20% Philips 20%
Elf	NNPC 60% Elf 40%
Texaco	NNPC 60% Texaco 20% Chevron 20%
Pan Ocean	NNPC 60% Pan Ocean 40%
NNPC	100% Government owned

Nigeria as at 2001 through the oil wells in the Niger Delta produces about 2.5 million barrels of oil per day. Using the 2001 prevailing market price of $25.00

per barrel, the cost of production comes to $3.5 per barrel for onshore while offshore is $5.00 per barrel. Put together, this amount to $4.25 as average for both onshore and offshore productions per barrel for the joint venture operator. This cost is borne by the joint venture operator who deploys capital for the operation. It is not borne by the government through NNPC. Some leaders claim oil fields are federal government investment. This is not true except where NNPC prospects directly for oil like it does through the Nigeria Petroleum Development Company (NPDC). In the end how do these companies make their money back, the fact is that at the end of the day, they have not invested anything.

By the terms of agreement, at the end of the day, the oil companies are paid the crude oil equivalent of their investment. So who judges the quantum of their investment? This is back to the era when the Europeans took away five gallons of palm oil for a small hand mirror in the same Niger Delta area through the activities of the Royal Niger Company. The oil companies pay into the Federal coffers, petroleum profit tax, royalty (about 20%), and crude oil tax, further 60% joint venture share is paid to NNPC, in all after the oil companies have deducted their cost, they are left with less than 20% of the total share.

Firstly, in terms of money;

2.3 million barrels of crude oil per day at $25.00 translates into:

2,300,000 X $25 = $57,500,000 per day that leaves the Niger Delta.
Converted to Naira at N122 to $1;

This amounts to N7, 015,000,000 per day.

168

This means that in 365 days, about two trillion, five hundred and sixty billion, four hundred and seventy five million Naira (N2, 560,475,000,000) leaves the Niger Delta.

Secondly, obtaining the cost of production from the oil companies;

2, 300,000 X $4.25 = $9, 775, 000 per day.

This amount is deducted from the amount made on daily basis before the rest is declared for sharing, this means that:

$57, 500,000 - $9, 775, 000 leaving $47, 725, 000 per for the company and government to share, meaning:

$47,725,000 x N122 x 365 = N2, 125,194,250,000 annually.

From this, the Federal Government receives the following

1).   Petroleum Profit Tax
2).   Royalty (see box on Shell account)
3).   VAT (5%)
4).   60% Joint-Venture share to NNPC.

If at the end of the year, the Oil Company is left with about 15% (assumption), then it would have made about N318, 778,936,500 as profit or $2,612,942,102 profits annually. The fact is that as long as the crude oil flows, the oil companies do not record losses as whatever it is they spend prospecting for oil is deducted as crude payment before anything is done. It means Shell which controls about 35% share in the oil industry carts away about 35% of the above profits.

From the leftover passed to the federal government after NNPC has also made its own deductions, the oil producing states are given 13% as derivation for the plunder of their land. It had been 1% hitherto before Gen. Ibrahim Badamosi Babangida made it 3% and finally, the 1999 constitution made it not less than 13%. If this were from 1970 till date (2003), this would mean that the Niger Delta area has contributed about:

Seventy one trillion, one hundred and twenty one billion, four hundred ten million, two hundred fifty thousand naira (N71, 121, 410, 250, 000) in thirty-three years.

The question is why use a flat figure knowing full well that these figures had fluctuated in the past. Due to inflationary trends, the standard of living today is not the same as it used to be. Today's one hundred and twenty two naira is equivalent to one Naira thirty years ago. So the flat rate is justified.

Life in the Niger Delta has deteriorated also to this tune which is the value of what it has given to the nation. Its youths have been wasted, its environment wasted, its resources wasted, yet the nation has nothing to show for it except for the leaders who themselves had become rich to the same tune that the nation had been plundered in collaborations with the oil corporations. The above calculations is only official figures, it is unfortunate that no record of these oil corporations' fraud on the nation, in their nefarious bunkering activities is yet available.

The Niger Delta and its people bear the loss of the gains of others. This has continued in over forty years of oil exploration in the area. The economic fraud on the Niger Delta continues just as the political fraud continues in the form of unabated tinkering with the unity of the people. These had been the vindictive political strategy of the Action Group in the West against the people of the
170

Niger Delta, the NCNC politics of enslavement in the East, the NPC politics of 'dominate them at all cost'. And the continuous divide and rule strategy of the oil companies using the weapon of 'community elder settlement' to suppress agitation and aid the federal government in the murder of various sons of the Niger Delta under the military era.

Traversing the entire Niger Delta one wonders how the often-truncated community development programmes of these oil corporations have helped any host community. The programmes are often not visible on ground as the people continuously live in abject poverty with no feasible means of livelihood. This has brought about hostage situations, monetary demand for compensation and the usual restiveness of the youths. The divide and rule tactics of the imperialist companies like Shell, Chevron, Mobil, Texaco, etc has ensured their continuous devastation and plunder of the Niger Delta.

These companies are quick at reeling out list of programmes carried out in their host communities. The truth in most cases is that these programmes have never translated into better life for the people within these host communities. Rather, they are creating within the same communities, traitors in the sons of the land who they can use to douse the agitation of the people as it was in Ogoniland where the aspirations of the people was halted with the murder of Saro-Wiwa.

It is a pity that while the Niger Delta rots away, sink deeper into poverty, lay completely in waste environmentally, the overlords smile away with the loots. Shell uses the profit to develop Dutch homeland, Chevron repatriates profit to further enrich the super rich U.S., Mobil swells the French pride and the Northern and other parts of Nigeria develop faster at unprecedented pace. It is annoying to see Lagos, Abuja, Minna, Enugu,

Kano and other cities develop at the expense of the Niger Delta and the area remains one large shanty reeling in untold hardship and poverty.

Tertiary institutions within the Niger Delta are infrastructurally deficient, not befitting tertiary standard. Universities of Minna, Lagos, Ife, Zaria, Nsukka, Ibadan, Abuja and others are just millenniums ahead of the ones in the Niger Delta. Yet the plundering of the beautiful bride must continue with the oil companies and federal government hunting the soul of Niger Delta. The federal government carts away about 85 percent of the loot in the form of royalty, petroleum profit tax, VAT, Joint Venture payment, etc while the rest goes to the oil companies. It should be stated here that gas exploration is the exclusive preserve of the federal government; no company has any stake in it.

The Niger Delta that generates so much for the nation sinks in poverty. Niger Delta is peopled by an army of jobless youths on whose shoulders rest the frustrating responsibility of liberating their future. The plunder continues and the government is richer for it. The oil companies swell in fortune, but the Niger Delta people bear the burden and the constraint of their well being. There is no single community in the Niger Delta area where life works so well. Communities within the Niger Delta are today far cruder environmentally than they were in pre-oil era owing to the activities of the oil corporations. There is no place in the Niger Delta where minimal comfort is provided.

The Niger Delta is a system in chaos and dilapidation. Its soul is at the brink of collapse, milked by strangers. If the oil wells in the area suddenly run dry, the oil multinational corporations would leave without losing a penny. The federal government would abandon it and focus on the agricultural sector or other viable sectors but the Niger Delta area would reel in the wake of both political, economic abandonment and disillusionment. Their land ravaged and their wealth plundered, their physical environment polluted, their waterways flowing with spilled crude oil and the people live on the edge. Now is the battle to save the soul of Niger Delta.

OIL COMPANIES/FG'S PLUNDERING OF THE NIGER-DELTA: A BRIEF LOOK INTO SHELL'S ACCOUNTS

SHELL'S ECONOMIC PERFORMANCE FOR YEAR 2002

719,000 Barrels per day of crude oil
812 million standard cubic feet of gas per day sold.

TRANSLATED:

Assuming crude oil price is at $25 per barrel on the average for 2002 and the cost of production is put at the average of $4.25 for both onshore and offshore.

719,000 X $25 = $17, 975, 000 per day
in 365 days, this means
$17, 975, 000 X 365 = $6, 560, 875, 000 (A)

COST OF PRODUCTION

719, 000 X $4.25 = $3, 055, 750
in 365 days, this means
$3, 055, 750 X 365 = $1, 115, 348, 750 (B)

Deduct B from A

$6, 560, 875, 000 - $1, 115, 348, 750
= $5, 445, 526, 250 (for year 2002)

This is the joint-venture profit share between SHELL and the JV partners. The federal government takes about 85% of this through joint venture partnership share, royalty, rent, petroleum profit tax, etc, leaving about 15% as profit for the oil companies.

SHELL'S COMMUNITY SUSTAINABLE DEVELOPMENT PROGRAMME IN THE NIGER-DELTA

In the year 2002, SHELL claimed to have spent $67, 000, 000 on community development programme.
This money is taken from the JV profit and expressed as a %age of profit.

$$\frac{\$67, 000, 000 \ X \ 100\%}{\$6, 560, 875, 000}$$

= 1.02% of total money generated before deductions. It becomes 1.2% if joint venture investments are deducted.

This 1.2 % is only deducted from the crude oil, if the gas sales are added; this thins down to a very insignificant figure. From the above, the propaganda that the oil companies are involved in community development in the Niger Delta in the light of the plundering insults the sensibility of the people whose environment is being daily degraded by the activities of these oil companies.

DEDUCING SHELL'S PROFIT

According to the 2000 MOU, companies receive a fixed amount per barrel of crude depending on market price. At $25.00, the companies would receive about $1. 15, this of course is after deducting production cost, which is $4.25.

$$719,000 \times \$1.15$$

$$\$826,850 \times 365$$
$$= \$301,\,800,\,205 \times N122$$
$$= N36,819,630,500$$

FG'S DEDUCTIONS

From this profit made by the company, the Federal

Government collects about 93% in forms of taxes,

royalties and equity shares.

ROYALTIES

- 20% for onshore production.
- 18 ½% for territorial waters and continental shelf areas up to 100 meters deep water.
- 16 2/3% for production in territorial waters and continental shelf beyond 100 meters depth.

NOTE: SHELL deducts it cost from the income in the form of crude payment and thus bears no risk according to the JV agreement. Thus, all costs are presumed removed before the above final figures are arrived at to get the profit the Oil Company makes at the expense of the lives of the Niger Delta people.

176

AMONGS THE PROJECTS (PHYSICAL)

INCLUDED IN THE $67,000,000 (JV)

PURPORTEDLY SPENT IN YEAR 2002 ARE:

1). Completion of 116 kilometers of community roads.
2). 21 rural electrification projects with 19 communities supplied electricity by adjoining SPDC flow-stations.
3). 2,600 secondary and 863 university scholarships.
4). Completion and donations of science labs to 3 community schools and giving science equipment to five others.
5). Donation of 120,000 text books to 70 secondary schools.
6). One riverine mobile clinic procurement.
7). Rehabilitated 32 water schemes and hand pumps.
8). Building three Women Development Centers.
9). Established 26 community based enterprises.

ENVIRONMENT:

SHELL claimed to have achieved a significant reduction in the number of oil spills incidences and volume of oil spills without the figures.

In gas flaring, flaring it claimed is down by 33%. That means the Niger Delta is still basking in the yoke gas flaring.

OIL EXPLORATION AGAINST COMMUNITY DEVELOPMENT PROJECTS IN THE LAST 3 YEARS

YEAR	COM. DEVT. FIG	OIL EXPLORATION
2000	$60 million	795,000b/d @$30per/b
2001	$63 million	837,000b/d@$30per/b
2002	$67 million	709,000b/d@$30per/b

NIGERIAN CONTENT CLAIM

The claims 3,200 contracts were awarded to local contractors, claiming this is about 80% of all contracts awarded.

The questions are what is the total value of these contracts? Are the 80% worth the same value as the 20% left? Are they major contracts or sub-contracts, i.e., contracts let to local contractors by other foreign contractors employed by SHELL?

FINAL NOTE:

The above is an example to give a glimpse into the picture of how the Niger-Delta has continued to be milked since oil was first discovered. Today, Oloibiri is a shadow of its old past with nothing to show for years of oil exploration. It is now confined to the relics of history.

The Niger Delta is decaying while the oil companies claim over-bloated achievements in community development, one wonders what is 1.2%

178

compared with the huge profit made by the imperial oil companies that pays slave wages to their Nigeria employees. The amount of money ploughed back into the Niger Delta is insignificant in relation to what is plundered. On the other hand, it would have been better for company like SHELL and the others to plough back as much as 70% of profit to better the Niger Delta.

SHELL is one of the numerous oil companies licensed to plunder the Niger Delta. They have continued the tradition of the colonialists plundering of the environment and appropriate profit to develop and enrich their home countries while the masses in the Niger Delta groan in poverty. These companies have been plundering the area since 1958. Whether these claimed development programs claimed by SHELL and other oil companies and even the Federal Government has translated into good lives for the people of the area remains a question for the people affected to judge.

PART FOUR

THE AGITATION AND AGITATORS
- SOVEREIGN NATIONAL CONFERENCE
- THAT NIGERIA MAY SURVIVE

CHAPTER TWELVE

<u>BRIEF HISTORY OF THE AGITATION</u>

The battle for the liberation of Niger Delta from the hold and domination of strange elements began with the ever resilient and amiable Oba Akenzua II of the Benin Empire. The royal father who ascended the throne of his fore fathers after Oba Ovoramwen, who had fought the British to a standstill against the appropriation of Edo land, was a champion of the course of the minority in the West. In the Eastern part, Sir Udo Udoma led the same course against the dominance of the Ibos over the Eastern minorities.

The royal father had vehemently protested the inclusion of the Benin and the Warri provinces in the West when the colonialist partitioned the Southern region into two with a decree in 1946. The learned royal father read between the acts and began agitation against it. This agitation led to the conference of the people of the Warri and Benin provinces in 1947. This was the year that the Yoruba Cultural group, the Egbe om' Oduduwa was formed in London by Awolowo. It must be stated here that some minority groups had formed various cultural associations that predate this association.

Some of these associations are today still functional since they did not translate into political parties like the now defunct Egbe Omo Oduduwa, the Jamiyar Mutanen Islamiyar and the Ibo States Union. An example is the Urhobo Progressive Union, which is still in existence today. The conference in Benin vehemently expressed the fear of domination of the minorities by the monolithic majority ethnic groups. Oba Akenzua stood in opposition to this other groups even though the Binis are culturally related to the Yorubas through the great Bini prince and founder of modern Yoruba states, Oduduwa and would have justified his adoption in the union.

In the East, the United Nigeria Independent Party led by Eyo Ita had become opposition to the NCNC in the parliament and sponsored agitation for the creation of Calabar Ogoja Rivers State for the minority in the East. This party aligned with the Action Group after Eyo Ita lost his control of the East in 1953. It should be noted here that the minorities in the West aligned against the Action Group that controlled the West with the NCNC while the Eastern minorities aligned with the same Action Group in the NCNC dominated Eastern part. The point is that the creation of the Midwest was actually not done because the NCNC supported the agitation of the minorities in the West. It was because the NCNC wanted to score a political victory and break the dominance of the Action Group in the West. The same NCNC had opposed the creation of similar state in the East, which the Action Group that had opposed the same in the West supported. The founding fathers fought for independence not in the same manner that the agitators for resource control within the Niger Delta have done.

The founding fathers were not killed and hounded into jails by the British like it is being done to the people of the Niger Delta even long after independence. They merely agitate for independence over cups of tea with the colonial authorities. They were over a long period of time, cronies of the colonial masters.

What then is the proof that this is not colonialism or jungle cannibalism where the lions feed on the soul of the squirrels within a supposed liberated nation or is this contraption called Nigeria a liberated jungle?   The
184

colonialists came, traded with the people of the Niger Delta with the various resources from here, this means that the region has for long been feeding European homelands with its resources. The same region has, in the last forty years, sustained a nation that had left it groping in the darkness of underdevelopment and environmental degradation.

THE SOVEREIGN NATIONAL CONFERENCE

The former President of the Nigeria, Chief Olusegun Obasanjo while answering a question on this issue (sic: SNC), in the presidential debate during his re-election campaign goofed. It was unfortunate that South-South (Niger Delta) sons and prominent journalists like Ray Ekpu and John Momoh who were among the panelists could not take him head on. They allowed him to have a field day as he derided the future of the nation as an unserious issue. The whole charade showed their own commitment to a matter that bothers on the soul of their own geopolitical zone.

In answering the question put to him on resource control and Sovereign National Conference, the president opined that he was not averse to SNC. In his answer he stated that if there must be a conference, it would not have a sovereign tag. Sovereignty he said belongs to the people who have elected him and others to represent them.

He further went on to say that any legislature that goes to pass votes on such a programme is not worth its onions. In another vein, he said none of the advocates of the SNC has a structure or format or even a candid reason for the cry. He said the elite cry marginalization when they fail to get what they want. The picture above gives one the impression that the former president, who is himself one of the elites of the country, has lost touch with his primary constituency, which is the grassroots. He has failed to see the reality on ground and his advisers were disillusioned eggheads. The marginalization is far among the poor masses than among the elite. It is the masses that have been economically, politically, socially, and infrastructurally cut off from the rest of the society in a nation they called their own. Perhaps a visit to the Niger Delta by the ex-president, I do not mean a visit to Port Harcourt, a visit to the hinterland will show him what Nigerians are suffering.

The former President and probably those around him who did not support the SNC were political jobbers. If the bad example set by the late Attorney General and Minister for Justice was what the president had in mind, then it is understandable. The basis for the struggle for some people was to gain political advantage and these are the kind of people that the nation must be wary about. Riding on the crest of a particular form of struggle to achieve political aim is not in itself all bad, but it is bad when one become an antagonist of the very system that catapulted one to that height.

The sovereign national conference must, if there must be any at all, conform to the people's demand. If any conference must hold, it must be a sovereign national conference. This will first and foremost recognized the political and economic sovereignty of the ethnic nationalities that are the component units of the nation. This fact has to first and foremost be acknowledged and impressed upon all that no tribe conquered the rest of the nation. Or do we now begin to feel especially in the Niger Delta, that the area was liberated from the Biafrans so that the area can become political and economic slave territory for the rest of the nation? Or should the Ibos begin to feel that after all they did not win the war and therefore have no right of co-existence within the union?

The word sovereignty cannot be removed from the conference. If this is done, it will become a mere 'Political Talk-shop' for egocentric idle politicians. A political talk-shop like the one the president is proposing holds no future for Nigerians. The sovereignty of the ethnic nationalities cannot be denied. It is true that the union was not contracted by any accord but by fraud and force. This is why the union must not continue to thrive by fraud and force.

Another question is representation. Should it to be proportional? That is, ethnic nationalities represented according to their population. Or should it be a representative per ethnic nationality? The question of representation should not be a problem or a threat to the SNC; it is the focus that matters. The representatives however configured are coming to defend the interest of their nationality within the union. The goal is to fashion out the reasons and conditions of our living together, not as conquered people but as a people deserving of each other's respect. This means that we must first and foremost be told why we must continue as a nation, then how we must continue as a nation and our individual interests within the nation. It would be these quasi-national interests that would in the end form the broad national interest and lead the nation on the path of true federalism and resource control. This is not a voting exercise where some would use their numerical advantage to suffocate opposing ideas in order to carry on with their enslavement.

Sovereignty truly belongs to the people. It can be taken and it can be given. In democracy, it is believed that democracy takes care of agitation. Democracy is not an alternative to Sovereign National Conference and resource control. It can only serve as the springboard. The question is, can the national assembly serve as SNC? No. The national assembly is an extension of the old order, brought about by the very same order, which it cannot seek to change. It can only restructure based on the aspiration of the people and then set the stage for the SNC.

SNC is meant to usher in a new history for the people. It is meant to discuss how we wish to be governed, not ruled and dominated like captured prisoners without rights. It is to discuss how we can exercise our rights within the union and not get killed by another citizen on the whims and caprices of religious bigotry. It is to discuss how the use of our resources will benefit us today and in the future without the proceeds ending in the private accounts of some slothful feudal lords. It is meant to discuss how our wealth can translate into good life for the entire nation. It is meant to discuss how everyone can actualize his potential without applying so much weight to drag others down.

SNC is meant to bring governance close to the people and make the leaders true servants of the people. It is meant to make everyone responsible and held accountable to the union without fear or favour to ethnic nationality, religious leaning, or political ideology. It is not interested in the past, or the present. It is interested in building a virile nation for the future generations. They should not experience this hate, anger and disgust that pervades the nation. It is meant to make us think first as Yoruba-Nigerian, Itshekiri-Nigerian, Hausa-Nigerian, Urhobo-Nigerian, Ijaw-Nigerian, Ibo-Nigerian, Ibiobio-Nigerian etc. It is to propel us to think Nigeria first so that we can have common ground of agreement that will enable us live together as one.

The SNC is meant to engender competition within the national polity so that all units can develop their own potential. It is meant to develop the individual, the family, the community, and the nation. Someone may say, we can achieve all these through constitution amendments. True, we have had several constitutions; they have not stopped the killings in all parts of the nation. It has not stopped the various political killings. It has not stopped ethnic agitation. It has not removed the distrust among the ethnic nationalities. Then, what has the constitution achieved for the nation but further chaos. After, the conference, regions can freely declare what kind of state they want to pursue within the union and vigorously pursue it so long it will not infringe on the right of the other nationalities. It is not a constitutional amendment that Nigerians want. It is a Sovereign National Conference of ethnic nationalities, the one that deals with all the questions of the basis of our coexistence within the nation that we proudly call ours.

JONATHAN'S NATIONAL CONFERENCE EXAMINED

The **2014 National Conference** was inaugurated by the Nigerian President Dr. Goodluck Ebele Jonathan on the 17th March, 2014 in Abuja, Nigeria. There were about 492 delegates selected to represent a cross-section of Nigerians including the professional bodies group. The Conference was headed by retired Chief Justice Idris Legbo Kutigi.

After a plenary session that lasted for weeks, the Conference was broken into 20 committees, viz: Public Finance and Revenue among others. All the 20 committees have submitted their reports to be deliberated upon at the next plenary session.

The principal Officers of the conference comprised of Chairman; Justice Idris Kutigi (Rtd), Vice Chairman; Prof. Bolaji Akinyemi and Secretary Dr. Valerie Azinge.

The following were also the main Committees: Devolution of Power Committee; Political Restructuring and Forms of Government; National Security; Environment; Politics and Governance; Law, Judiciary, Human Rights and Legal Reform; Social Welfare; Transportation; Agriculture; Society, Labour and Sports; Public Service; Electoral Matters, Foreign Policy and Diaspora Matters; Land Tenure Matters and National Boundary; Trade and Investment Committee; Energy; Religion; Public Finance and Revenue Generation; Science, Technology and Development Immigration.

In inaugurating a national conference, Goodluck Jonathan is the first Nigerian leader that agreed in principle that the basis of co-existence needed to revisited and discussed. He demonstrated that even the leaders of this nation know that there is everything wrong in the way we are configured, even though for some selfish reasons they fail to take bold steps to correct this anomaly and put this nation on the path to true greatness which is the dream of every Nigerian.

The Obasanjo administration set up the Ogomudia committee which was to look into the reasons for minority uprising during his time but rather than take and implement what were the recommendations of the committee, Obasanjo buried it and decided that the Niger-Delta has had enough and brutal force was rather used to quell all restiveness and agitation emanating from the region. At least he also knew that there was problem in the nation that needed solution but he had other plans.
190

At the inauguration of the national conference, the president's speech shows that he and every other leader of this country knows that there is great fault at the foundation of this country. His resolve to have a national conference may not have been underscored by the menace of Boko Haram and the MEND in the Niger-Delta, these have become hydra-headed problems for the nation.

In looking at the Jonathan's national dialogue, a lot of things seem to have worked against it and it is greatly doubted that anything would come out of its recommendations. One wonders if it was not an attempt to play the second tenure card that the president decided on a national dialogue. A lot of the factors that would militate against this money wasting venture are:

1. Once Jonathan lost his attempt as second term president, we might have seen the end of the report of that committee; whoever comes in may do well to sweep the recommendations under the carpet.

2. The National Conference has no sovereign tag to it. This shows that Goodluck Jonathan is not different from all the other leaders who see themselves as the elected sovereigns of the people therefore the people cannot have another sovereign.

3. If the opposition party comes to power, the money spent on convening a national conference would have become wasted as they would obviously scrap the reports since they did not participate in it.

4. The Goodluck Jonathan National Conference can best be described as political conference of selected elder statesmen. All the participants were selected by the presidency

and the people did not have any input in deciding who represented them.

5. A lot of ethnic nationalities were not adequately represented, what we need in Nigeria is a sovereign conference of ethnic nationalities, not a conference of elder statesmen and professionals.

6. The sovereign national conference must not be politically motivated or created so that some elder statesmen can have a taste of the national cake, it must be patriotically motivated and the representatives must be true representatives of their ethnic nationalities selected by their people to represent their interest.

7. All ethnic nationalities, large or small must be represented on equal basis not proportional representation.

8. The conference of Jonathan had no go areas; a sovereign national conference should have no go areas. Ethnic nationalities should be given the freedom to decide if they want to continue to be part of a union that makes them second class citizens and squander their resources.

9. The conference recommendations must be binding on all the leaders, all the sectors, all the political parties and all the citizens of the nation, the document arising from a sovereign national conference must form the basis of our co-existence and not some money wasting ventures that would end up in the trash bin of our political elites.

10. Finally, the documents resulting from a sovereign national conference would be devoid of any political influence, only the

people can through a referendum vote to modify any part thereof.

We have deceived ourselves in this nation for so long. We have been given the impression that some people can do whatever they like in the country and get away with it while some people do not even have the right to own their father's land. They are slaves in the scheme of things within the nation. The truth is if Sokoto, Kano, Katsina and Zamfara can practice sharia law within their states in a circular country, why will Delta, Bayelsa, Rivers not be allowed to determine how people can live within their state by stating the terms and condition for owning the oil fields.

If all the farmlands in the North belong to the people and they decide how to plant, what to plant and yet again get government subsidized fertilizer to grow their crops and yet they decide how much to sell their crops even to government agencies, why will the same not be allowed to happen in the Niger-Delta by allowing the people decide what price tag to place on the oil found on their soil. The terms of ownership of the offshore oil can be decided, between the states and the federal government.

This is why we need a sovereign national conference to correct some of these anomalies and readdress how we live within this forced union called Nigeria. The oil resources on the soil of Oloibiri is no more and the town is no better for it. Oloibiri is now a relic for the national oil museum. It does not look like there was oil ever drilled on Oloibiri soil that is the aftermath under-developing the Niger Delta. The rest of the nation is busy under-developing the Niger-Delta, not correcting it now would spell doom for the future of the region as the minority ethnic nationalities do not have a place in the nation called Nigeria.

These are some of the reasons why the Goodluck Jonathan national conference was not the solution or the body to chart a new direction for the national and show us the basis of our co-existence. We need more than a political talk-shop of selected elder statesmen to right the wrongs of our co-existence. History beckons on our leaders, today and tomorrow to build this nation or leave it to its destruction.

CHAPTER THIRTEEN

<u>THE AGITATION</u>

When the issue of youth restiveness is discussed, the Niger Delta easily comes to mind. The fact remains that this is not an issue, for the Niger Delta alone but for the entire nation. It is not only the Niger Delta that has been restive. The nation has been restive since independence. Every part of the nation has been restive. It is just that the restiveness in the Niger Delta is the struggle of a people for the soul of their land. In other parts of the country, the restiveness has been against the agitation for fairness.

The maximum rulers and leaders have sought to keep this agitation under check by militarizing the South-South zone so that the plunder of their land can go on. So why is Niger Delta the only zone to be militarized if the entire nation is agitating for different forms of justice? Why is it the only zone that stirs the concern of the rulers while the lives of innocent citizens are freely taken in other parts of the nation?

There have been quite a number of violent riots in the nation since independence. There has indeed been no year without riots and violent protests. The North has the most shares of these violent riots, which are most times unnecessarily provoked. In each of the republics, as much as during military administrations, there has been destruction of lives and property, without the nation bating an eyelid. It was in protest of such killings that the nation engaged in civil war. Yet, the civil war has not stopped this. After the civil war, the nation helplessly looked away from the cause of the war. The nation has not address the cause of the war. After the 1999, elections again, militant ethnic organizations emerged to champion ethnic agenda. This has further buttressed the fact that Nigeria is time bomb waiting to explode.

A look into some of the riots that had been recorded within the nation will help:

- In 1966, Araba genocide in Sokoto, an entire congregation of Christians and southerners were wiped out in Sokoto Cathedral.
- Between 1963 and 1967, several thousands of Southerners were killed, maimed and mutilated in the North, leading to the civil war.
- In Kaduna (Rigasa), Northerners killed several Christians in religious riots.
- In year 2000, over 1000 Christians and Southerners were killed in the Sharia riots.
- In 1980, the Maitasine fanatics killed over 1000 Southerners, Moslems and Christians alike.
- Between 1981 and 1985, over 5,000 people (Southerners) were killed in Bauchi in religious onslaught.
- In Yola, more than a thousand people were slaughtered.
- Ilorin witnessed several religious riots in 1976, 1984, and 1986 where several Christians were killed.
- In 1995, soldiers sacked Ogoniland (Niger Delta), killing, maiming and raping people. Over 1000 people were killed.
- In year 2000, soldiers invaded Odi (Niger Delta), killing over 1,200 people.

NOTE: These are just few of the carnage perpetrated on Southerners in the North. In the same vein, the riots in the South have never been directed against the North except in few but rare reprisal attacks. The killings in the Niger Delta have been more of military invasions on the conquered people.

Then, why is it the Niger Delta agitation that has elicited so much passion? The reasons seem to be that the Niger Delta produces 90% of Nigeria's earning in crude oil. Outside that, production of cassava in Delta State makes Nigeria one of the world-leading producers of cassava. Presently, this staple food is the commonest food in Nigeria. So, the Niger Delta produces Nigeria's most vital food as well as its oil. There are also the investments of the multinational oil corporations within the Niger Delta worth billions of dollars. These are usually at stake when the youths become very restive as they vent their frustration on the system.

It is a wonder that the youths within the ethnic nationalities in the Niger Delta have over the years turned against themselves in the fight for independence while the land had been continuously plundered by strangers. The ethnic nationalities had lived in peace for centuries trading and inter-marrying with one another without these inter-ethnic wars and riots. Thus within the Niger Delta, there were no ethnic subjugation or domination. The people were good neighbors.

The advent of the colonialists changed all that. The freedom of the people was removed and a strange lordship declared over the people. However, this is not the issue, the issue is that the tribes must resolve their differences and be united for a common course. The enemy is not themselves. The fight is not the struggle for tribal expansionism or ethnic lordship over territories that the groups have cohabiting for centuries. The fight is not the battle for hostage taking or settlement from the oil companies.

The youths have to be determined to negotiate a better deal rather than killing one another and demand ransom from the oil companies. The generations past have failed and their collaboration with the imperialist multinationals have mortgaged the future of the youths. Most royal fathers scurry for the favor of the oil companies and in the process mortgage their domain and that of their future for annual peanuts from the companies. The youths presently must cut a new deal for the future generations.

The problem is growing daily and it is getting tougher. Life in the Niger Delta is becoming more difficult on daily basis. It is as if there are deliberate obstacles placed on the people. The system places greater limitations on the youths in the Niger Delta. The system creates more barriers that peace has eluded the area. With peace and unity in the area, the struggle for resource control becomes more cohesive. The target will become easier and faster to reach with unity of purpose amongst the people. It is unfortunate that the youths in the Niger Delta bear the greater brunt of the brutality in the system.

He has more obstacles to face. When his land flows with oil, it instantly with meager or no compensation, becomes the property of the federal government. His means of livelihood is thus taken away from him. His right to fish within the creeks is taken away with oil spillages. He gasps everyday for good air to breathe but exploration activities deny him his right to this. His land is declared unfit for human habitation but fit for the production of the crude oil that has enriched the rest of the nation.

He has no access to good and qualitative education. Even when he struggles to attain higher education, he is compelled to wait as the quota from his area had been over stretched. He is asked to wait until others catch up with him. The frustration of a harsh environment made worse by the fact that this same government is the gold mine of others within the nation. When his frustration is expressed, half measure that provides cut and nail solutions are provided and the system expects him to be grateful to it for the plunder of his homeland. This is a total rape of his homeland.

The homeland has not been helped by the caliber of leaders that had stood to fight for resource control. Some have used it only to score political victory and turn against the battle once this is achieved. Others turned to the fight only as vendetta against the system that had been cruel to their selfish ambition. Some are outright protagonists of the people's wish conniving with the system to betray true fighters. These were the people that betrayed Isaac Adaka Boro, Kenule Saro-Wiwa and others who died in the struggle. They were the same set that must see that Governor Victor Attah and Governor James Ibori and Governor Achike Udenwa never succeed in the fight for resource control and true federalism.

The youths must join in the new dawn of national unity, a new dawn to work out a better deal for the ethnic nationalities. The struggle has just begun and the people must put aside all differences and face a common course. The people of the Niger Delta, the Ijaws, the Urhobos, Itshekiris, Kalabaris, the Anangs, Ibiobios, Ogojas, Edos, all must be united in the battle for the soul of the Niger Delta. It will be a national liberation of the masses, politically and economically. This is not armed struggle.

It is the struggle of will and for justice like Nelson Mandela did in South Africa. The nation must be forced down to the Niger Delta if the nation refuses to come to Niger Delta. We cannot continue in this strangulation of the nation by re-circulation of the old order.

Ethnic agitation has also not been absent in other parts of the nation. Conflicts that seem to rock the very foundation of our coexistence have been known to occur in other parts of the nation. The West through the activities of youths had witnessed violent agitation, so is the North. The North has witnessed more uprising against other ethnic nationals than any other part of the nation. The West has witnessed great political upheavals, not targeted against any tribe or nations until recently, but against political manipulations of an unfair order. All these boil down to the fact that we have not understood the bases of our national coexistence.

The upheavals in the Niger Delta had never been against the rest of the nation neither has it been against any particular ethnic nationality but against an oppressive system or tendency. It has been against the ploy to keep the people in perpetual slavery. It had been a struggle against an order that enthrones strange feudal lordship on the people. It is a struggle to understand the basis of our coexistence within a nation that recognizes the importance of the region only because it sustains the rest of the nation.

Jobless soldiers should be used for more productive ventures and so are the nation's prisoners who feed on the nation without giving back to it rather than dissipate their energies on curtailing restive youths fighting for justice. The military as it is done in China should be engaged in various productive activities like farming. Promotion should be regulated to avoid producing spineless generals who have only fought wars
200

against the nation's treasury and the Niger Delta youths. Arms should be redistributed to avoid concentration like it was done in old USSR. Then it would be possible to check the ambition of overzealous officers who confuse process of change for chaos within the nation polity.

An SNC at this time as is being agitated is necessary to correct all the ills in the old order. It is needed to usher in a new order for the nation. The result of the SNC will be the ultimate contract between the ethnic nationalities, first among themselves and second, with the government. This ultimate accord will be the guiding principle of peaceful coexistence for a new and united Nigeria. It will be its guarding principle, its constitution or a guard to a true constitution. No tribe, no tongue, no people, no religion, will override its content. It will be the cord binding the nation together. A breach on one is a breach on all. Everyone will resist such breach to undermine the indivisibility of the union.

Then every part of the nation can lay equal claim to its development and contributes equally to it. Every nationality can be truly Nigerian. Every man will be equal irrespective of religion, social background or ethnic nationality. Nigeria will truly be the Nigeria that all desire rather than what the Europeans desired and gave to us. It will be a nation built and conceived by the people directly affected. Not the one built with the spilling of the blood of Africans through European expansionist agenda and the conspiracy of slavery. This now translates, in the present pre-colonial times, into economic and political enslavement, even of blacks on blacks as directed by the ex-colonialists. This enslavement was the agenda left by the colonialists as ploy to keep us in perpetual slavery.

That agenda was never for the freedom of Africa. The agenda was to make Africa remain in perpetual slavery. They left and handed over the mantle of economic slavery to their goons. They, in case of Nigeria, made it a grand design to keep the over ambitious South under the slavery of the feudalistic North. The oil companies have freely promoted this agenda in their activities. Now the time has come for change and this they resist. The Niger Delta, nay, Nigeria must save her soul from this bondage. Everyone including the leaders must move along with the sweeping change. It is a duty everyone owes to the nation.

THE ROLE OF THE MULTINATIONALS

The multinational oil corporations like Shell, Chevron and Mobil have in no small measure contributed to youth restiveness in the Niger Delta. It should be noted that these three between them prospects more than 1.5 million barrels of oil per day from the area. Shell alone controls more than forty five percent of oil explorations in the zone. These companies had often in the time past resorted to divide and rule tactics to break the ranks of the youths.

With the advent of the Europeans, the Royal Niger Company controlled the trade in the same region, like these oil companies today, the deal had often been that the RNC paid royalty to the families, communities, kingdoms whose properties or land were used. Apart from the royalty, they also provided protection for that community against external attack.

The advent of the oil companies saw a new wave of slavery been perpetrated on the people. For long the people had been passive, owing to their low level of education. The passivity of the people had been construed to mean their acceptance of slavery as the companies plundered the land and gave nothing in return. This they

202

did, in collaboration with strangers to the environment that in the name of federal government control the resources of a people they knew little or nothing about.

As the people began the process of agitation against perceived injustice against their land, the federal government and these companies decided to kill and silence all agitators so the enslavement can continue. Shell and the oil companies introduced a new dimension to it. They began to settle ghost workers within the communities rather than provide employment for the youths. They used these to quell any form of agitation. They also made monetary offers to the elders within the communities who help nip the agitation in the bud.

Another thing is the usual bogus claims of consistent effort at community development by these oil companies. Most times these claims amount to nothing compared to the billions they make from the region. The claims become more spurious against the background that the money they expend on these projects are joint venture money which means that NNPC still contributes about sixty percent of the money so, who really picks the bill?
The cottage industries, markets built, schools renovated, scholarships, cottage hospitals and so on are overtly publicized to give the impression that they are giving back to the communities where in actual fact most of these communities reek in poverty. They bribe community and youth leaders to kill genuine agitation against the enslavement of their land. Even in the award of contracts, the locals are the least considered. Nigerians are slaves when it comes to that. Faceless whites with little or no qualification boss even highly qualified Nigerians.

In the case of Chevron, it is even worse as Nigeria has almost been Americanized. Even drinking water is imported from America by Chevron. Jobs are good for

Nigerians only if there are no Americans or European firms to do the jobs. Chevron had been severally accused of arming the youths in the Niger Delta against one another. That is the American way of settling crisis. The world can be held to a standstill at gunpoint as long as the life of an American is not involved.

For Chevron, the region should be declared a dominion of the U.S as has become the fate of Iraq today. This is why most of their workers can stay in Lagos and come to work daily in chartered crafts in the region. The area is not fit for their habitation, only good enough to earn them the required dollars. To them the youths in the Niger Delta can waste themselves as long as the oil wells are not tampered with. The oil wells are more valuable than the people or their land or their future.

These companies and all the others aid the federal government to defraud the people. Aid it to degrade the environment and aid it to embezzle the funds because the companies themselves are frauds. It is very likely that the companies also defraud the government of the federation with the connivance of the officials of the government in bunkering activities. The NNPC has become helpless in checking the activities of joint venture operators who bask in the glory of spending the nation's money miserly on non-productive programmes and over-publicize such to boost their public image. They have taken the glory in community development efforts while only a miserly amount is actually spent by them.

They claim to be developing the Niger Delta while actually impoverishing the region. They take away the means of economic empowerment from the people as a means to keep them in perpetual slavery. The activities of the traditional rulers within the region who had become errand boys to these oil companies are so pathetic. They degrade the very culture they swore to uphold and of which they are custodians.

They are anathema to the very course that Jaja of Opobo fought, that Nana of Itshekiri fought, that Oba Ovoramwen fought, that Oba Akenzua II fought, that Kenule Saro-Wiwa fought. These are the gluttonous generation that the youths must rebel against. They have sold and appropriated the very soul of the Niger Delta. They have traded the culture handed to them to protect for plates of porridge on the white man's table. They are drunk with the soul of their subjects, aiding the oil companies to lay waste, the kingdoms once prosperous, as handed to them by the forefathers.

MEASURES OF ENSLAVEMENT AND INFERIORITY COMPLEX

For too long the Niger Delta region has been treated with measures that served to further impoverish the region and make the indigenes feel inferior in the scheme of things within the system. Yet when the white man first stepped foot on the Niger Area, it was in the Niger Delta area.

The region has been treated since independence like a conquered region within the union. This is not surprising, the Europeans realized very early in the day that the area wielded so much enormous wealth and the only way to perpetrate a legacy of looting was to keep the people underdeveloped.

In pre-independent Nigeria, a legacy that makes the people within the Niger Delta inferior to the rest of the regions seem to have been consciously developed. The area is thus one leprous zone needing special attention. Half measures to cure it of this leprous infection had thus been variously designed.

In 1962, the Abubakar Tafawa Balewa administration gave the Niger Delta Development Board (NDDB) which in the end did nothing to change the lives of the people. The people became the more impoverished as a result of this while the nation was getting richer.

The Babangida administration came with the Oil Mineral Production Area Development Commission (OMPADEC); it was another avenue to siphon the nation's wealth. This board was replaced by the Petroleum Trust Fund of the Abacha administration. In the Democratic dispensation of Chief Olusegun Obasanjo, the name of the programme changed to Niger Delta Development Commission.

These programmes have never gone beyond the tarring/grading of roads within the region as if this is the only problem that the region faces. The same pattern of half measure health care, rural electrification, water supply and usually outrageously expensive consultancy services are rendered. These programmes have never gone to empower the people economically or politically as a people with the same right as the rest of the tribes within the Nigeria nation. It has become the usual norm to use these programmes to keep the people busy while the legacy of plunder by the system goes on.

People who have neither vision nor any insight into the problems of the area design these programmes and foist on the people. They are rather meant to make the people feel grateful to their conquerors who have been so benevolent to give them the chance to serve the slave masters. Over the years, it has thus been consciously inculcated into the psyche of the average Niger Deltan that he is so disadvantaged within the union that he needs special attention to enjoy the wealth found within his region to which he has no right.

As the government designs these programmes so the oil companies design mediocre measure called community development measures. These measures in the same way duplicate duties of the government programmes. The host communities are thus expected to be grateful for the years of environmental waste, resources plunder, and economic impoverishment that their area has been subjected as slaves of the slave masters.

In the early days of the Nigeria contraption, Chief Obafemi Awolowo did not need a special Cocoa Development Commission to develop the old Western Region. Dr. Nnamdi Azikiwe did not need a special Oil Palm Development Commission to develop the old Eastern Region neither did Sir Ahmadu Bello need a special Groundnut Board to develop the Northern Region.

Yet all the legacies built by these people within their region are the basis of comparison in today's Nigeria. The culture changed when it came to the Niger Delta as the resources were annexed and a legacy of plunder and neo-colonial enslavement began. The people are consciously rejecting these measures now. This resistance is equally being rejected by the very system that perpetrates these measures.

It is however a fact that when a change is due to be effected, those who stand in the way of such changes are soon swept along by the change. It is either they become apostles of such change or they become confined to portion of history that only recognizes them as reactionary elements within the change. The Niger Delta, nay, the Nigerian masses are calling for a change and the leaders can no longer pretend that these are blind agitation.

The psyche of the people of the Niger Delta people has become so damaged that it has become imperative for the average Niger Deltan to see himself as one that is insignificant within the system. The relevance he has of course is the oil that flows within his region. He thus must need a specially constituted body to give him stipends from the loot and plunder going on within his region.

The Niger Deltan leader is only good as a third class citizen and as errand boys of the same very feudal system that has annex all his resources. These are conscious measures of enslavement to perpetrate the looting of the area. Like slaves that worked the American plantations in the era of slave trade, the Niger Delta must be led in military chains while the feudal lords supervise the flogging of the people into line through the guns and armored tanks.

These short terms measures of placating the Niger Delta must be rejected for real developmental programmes that will ensure a great future for the area. A better developmental programme that will ensure that the future is not mortgaged as has been done in the past by opportunistic leaders in the guise royal-hood must now be negotiated. It is time the area is moved away from this rot that the system has placed it.

CHAPTER FOURTEEN

<u>THE AGITATORS, DEAD AND LIVING</u>

In the struggle for resource control, one cannot but talk about the contributions of his royal highness, Oba Akenzua II who was actually the rallying force towards the movements for minority right leading to the creation of the Midwestern region. Sir Udo Udoma was also among the warriors. So were the likes of Dennis Osadebey, Jereton Mariere of the Urhobo Progress Union. However, the rage for the liberation of the soul of the Niger Delta goes with tribute to the martyrs.

Also in the battle for SNC, so many Nigerians like Chief M. K. O Abiola died trying to actualize a mandate freely given by Nigerians as expressed in June 12. While some have lost the steam, others have remained steadfast in their call for an SNC. Events in Nigeria in the past ten to fifteen years have done nothing but bring us closer to the truth; the nation needs an SNC to remain a truly great nation. In the battle for SNC, the contribution of Major Gideon Orka cannot but be mentioned.

Though he had sought the wrong means to achieving a good goal, he had by his coup brought to the fore, the fact that the nation was a contraption of a wrong configuration. He made Nigerians to realize that we indeed needed to talk to decide if we were actually meant to live together. His coup was a wrong approach at correcting a political problem. It was also ill timed, though his visions were good.

At this time, the seed had been sown, or rather; an issue long suppressed had been brought to the fore. Moreover, the people in the Niger Delta had begun to feel the heat as their land was constantly being raped and plundered with nothing to show for the plunder. The minorities were simply the binding factor for the majority tribe. They were the cords that held Nigeria together.

From the advent of the Europeans, it was obvious that the Niger Delta was the Father Christmas of the nation. Amalgamation was necessary only as long as the minority Niger Delta groups were there to provide the needed lifeline for the survival of the nation. The Royal Niger Company began the plundering, the colonialist extended it, and the system handed down at independence perfected the looting.

So many people have died while fighting against this looting. Others living have carried. Each day the battle is gathering momentum. Those who were killed to suppress the agitation have long after been vindicated by the system. Yet others must continue, as if all is well. To some of the fallen and living ones, honour deserved.

Isaac Adaka Boro:
Major Isaac Jasper Adaka Boro (September 10, 1938 – May 9, 1968), fondly called "Boro", was a celebrated Niger Delta nationalist and Nigerian civil war hero. He was one of the pioneers of minority rights activism in Nigeria.
In his autobiography, "The Twelve-Day Revolution", Boro wrote about his early life:
"I am reliably informed that I was born at the zero hour of twelve midnight on 10 September 1938, in the oil town of Oloibiri along humid

creeks of the Niger Delta. My father was the headmaster of the only mission school there. Before I was old enough to know my surroundings, I was already in a city called Port Harcourt where my father was again the headmaster of another mission school. This was in the early forties. The next environment where I found myself was in my home town, Kaiama. My father had been sent there to head a school yet again."

He was many parts and different things to different people - a university students' leader, a teacher, policeman and Nigerian army officer. An undergraduate student of chemistry and student union president at the University of Nigeria, Nsukka, he left school to lead an armed protest against the exploitation of oil and gas resources in the Niger Delta areas which benefitted mainly the federal government of Nigeria and a remote Eastern Nigeria regional government. He believed that the people of the area deserved a fairer share of proceeds of the oil wealth. He formed the Niger Delta Volunteer Force, an armed militia with members consisting mainly of his fellow Ijaw ethnic group.

Boro declared the Niger Delta Republic on February 23, 1966 and gallantly battled the Federal forces for twelve days. He was finally routed by the far superior Federal firepower. Boro and his compatriots were jailed for treason. However, the federal regime of General Yakubu Gowon granted him amnesty on the eve of the Nigerian civil war in May 1967. He enlisted and was commissioned as a major in the Nigerian army. He fought on the side of the Federal Government but was killed under mysterious circumstances in active service in 1968 at Ogu (near Okrika) in Rivers State.

"Today is a great day, not only in your lives, but also in the history of the Niger Delta. Perhaps it will be the greatest day for a very long time. This is not because we are going to bring heaven down, but because we are going to demonstrate to the world what and how we feel about oppression. Before today, we were branded robbers, bandits, terrorists or gangsters but after today, we shall be heroes of our land. For this reason, and for the good name of the Niger Delta People, do not commit atrocities such as rape, looting or robbery. Whatever people say, we must maintain our integrity. Moreover, you know it is against our tradition to mess about with women during war. You have been purified these many days. Be assured that if you do not get yourselves defiled within the period of battle, you shall return home safe even if we fail".

Isaac Adaka Boro and his men fought the first battle against the system long before Ojukwu declared the civil war against the same system. They sew the seed of agitation. His body was only recently relocated to the Niger-Delta from Lagos to be buried in Bayelsa State. It is a name the system has sought to bury in the sand of history. Isaac led the first insurrection to free the minority homeland from the hold of the monolithic Eastern government controlled by the same NCNC that had granted autonomy to the minorities in the West which was controlled by the AG.

Isaac in a twelve-day battle engaged the nation to liberate the Ijaws from the hold that the colonialists had subjected them to. He fought against the system so that the Ijaw nation could control their God given resources. He led an insurrection against the system in 1966 long
212

before the secessionist agenda of Biafra. Isaac had seen the slave-master relationship upon which the nation was built and was willing to liberate his people from the unfair equation as arranged by the colonialists.

He was a student leader as well as a fighter against the British fraud, which ensured that the minorities were slaves to the contraption they had put together. Though Isaac is dead today, but almost forty years after, time has proven that Isaac was fighting a just course. He died in the twelve days siege, put down by the guns of the same federation that had long maintained the slave-master relationship between the Niger Delta and Nigeria. This young man deserves the honour of a hero.

Today, the Niger Delta is under threat. The area is being plundered and very soon it would become another abandoned monument like the pyramids of Egypt. Only this time, the abandoned monuments will be monuments without aesthetic pleasures. They would be monuments of environmental degradation when the plunderers leave. Everyday brings one closer to the realities of what Isaac saw in his fight against the system. The Niger Delta is indeed battling to save itself from looters and plunderers. The soul of this young man still stirs in the grave as the soul of Niger Delta stirs in chain.

To the undiscerning eyes, Isaac may have lost the battle and the people may have returned home but in truth, the battle that Isaac Adaka Boro started still rages on, the people are still long on the battle field. Boro might be dead but the battle is not dead, several generals have been raised while some have died fighting on, others are taking up the mantle of its leadership. It has been a long day since 1966 but for sure *victoria ascerta*.

Kenule Saro-Wiwa:

The battle for the soul of Niger Delta cannot be complete without talking about the man Ken Saro-Wiwa. When Saro-Wiwa was murdered, the nation, nay, the world groaned. A brilliant son of the nation had been killed. Saro-Wiwa fought a just course without the power of gun against the guns of the system. His only weapon was his brilliance and the talent that nature had endowed him with. Yet the system could not bear the likes of him. He stood for the truth. He stood for his people.

The liberation of the Ogonis was what he gave his life for. His own people were the very tools used to set him up by the very system he sought to liberate them from. Kenule was an environmentalist, a writer and a leader of his people. He had a vision of an Ogoni nation, not a separate and distinct nation from Nigeria but within a just and equitable federation. He sought to cut a fair deal for his people from the system and the oil companies that were plundering Ogoni land.

Saro-Wiwa it was that brought the attention of the international community to the plight of the Niger Delta through the activities of the Movement for the Survival of Ogoni People. He used the elections of June 12 1993 to make the nation and the world listen and know that indeed, a big fraud was being perpetrated in the Niger Delta. For this course, Ken gave his life on the 10th of November 1995 when the regime of General Abacha murdered him.

As Saro-Wiwa fought to liberate his people, the same people were used to hang him. The very same people that he sought to cut a better deal for within the nation. The same people whose survival within the unbalanced nation called Nigeria he sought to negotiate. Saro-Wiwa had a vision of a better Ogoni land where the land is productive, where the citizens are coequals within

214

the larger Nigerian nation. And not a nation where the relevance of his people were tied to the crude oil they produced for the nation from which, they have nothing to show except poverty and environmental ruins.

The same people whose lands were being devastated and plundered by the oil companies, the same people that would more than him be the beneficiaries of a better deal. They were the very weapons of the system. These were people whose pockets are their immediate gains and the same elements within the people that would never want to live to see the dreams of the Wiwas and the Boros come true for a truly liberated Niger Delta within the Nation, Nigeria. He gave his soul for the struggle and the struggle has gained more momentum after him. Mention must be made of the eight others that were murdered with him. They gave their souls for the struggle to liberate their people.

June 12, 1993:

One cannot but personify the event of this day. It was the first time that Nigerians came out to think Nigeria first by putting away ethnic affiliation, religious leaning and regional bias to truly behave as Nigerians. It was the unity of the common man. It was the first time the masses were united and they took their destinies in their hands. They voted and did peacefully. It was the election that led to the realization of the fact that the nation had not been one after all. It was the election that would expose the fact that a part of the nation has actually enthroned itself as the real colonial masters over the rest.

The election won by Chief MKO Abiola was annulled just because he was not born to rule. The North could not consider a shift in power without negotiating. The votes of fourteen million Nigerians were voided by

General Ibrahim Badamosi Babangida without explanation save for the fact that some people in the North did not want Abiola to rule them even though Nigerians had voted for him. Chief MKO fought to keep his mandate for which he was murdered in jail. He died and June 12 died.

As he died, so did Alhaja Kudirat Abiola, the wife of the Chief who fought gallantly to liberate the people and help actualize a stolen mandate. Her unwavering resolve brought to the fore, the need for SNC. Her resolve hunted the military that soon cut her down. They killed her but she had contributed her lot to the struggle for an idea whose time had come and was fast becoming entrenched.

Pa Alfred Rewane also died for the course of the struggle. June 12 had so many casualties who had paid for our collective freedom. Yet their contribution is being swept under the carpet. It is as if what they fought for had been overtaken by events – the attainment of DEMOCRACY in 1999. The attainment of democracy has not removed the problem because June 12 in the first place did not create it. And thus, June 12 may have died but the ingredients, which remain salient to national unity, still linger. Chief Abiola may have died and so were the mandate and the sovereignty of the masses.

The sovereignty of Nigerians died and so was their mandate. Chief Abiola was June 12, and June 12 was Chief MKO Abiola. He died and the mandate died. Though June 12 died as did Chief Abiola but it had left an indelible print on the Nigeria polity. It has continued to open up the questions for the basis for our collective coexistence as a nation. Chief Abiola and Alhaja Kudirat were the lambs sacrificed on the altar of our pseudo-unity. The Nigeria masses saw in June 12, personified by

Chief Abiola, their liberation, unity and believe in one Nigeria. Unfortunately, the system had other plans.

The masses had no right to decide. The system as fraudulent as it is, must decide for them and so it decided that Chief Abiola was not the right man. Liberation was yet not ripe for the people. The system robbed the people of their mandate and that robbery had brought the greater agitation for SNC. Though June 12 and the Chief are dead, their contribution to the liberation of the people lives on.

QUOTES FROM LIVING AGITATORS

The above were those that ignited the flame of the agitation against a system that sought to enslave the Niger Delta and using the minorities as the binding factor of the nation. it is a glaring fact that the monolithic tribes have a common goal in the total devastation of the Niger Delta from which the tribes of the South had begun to opt out lately.

The death of the likes of Saro-Wiwa and every other person that had died in the pursuance of justice had not gone in vain. The battle has gathered greater momentum. More indigents of the region are becoming converts for the battle to liberate their homelands. Everyday has seen the rise in ranks of agitators given vent by the backing of fearless individuals that are mounting the saddles of political leadership in the area. It has become a sin against the people for their leaders to speak against the agitation.

Some leaders rode on the crest of this populist demand to endear themselves to their people even though they were also conspirators in the wanton looting of the wealth of the nation,

Chief James Onanefe Ibori: (former Governor of Delta State, 1999-2007)

"I am proud and I will continue to be proud, I will walk with my head high to know that I have personalities, elders, youths, political leaders, elected officials that are totally committed to this course. We will be beaten back, but we will not be at retreat, we have been called names, some have even said that the political leadership is engaged in this because they want to use it as a political platform.

We will once again take our destinies in our own hands and by the grace of God, history will judge us. For those of us elected, we have the electorate watching us very closely, one day; you will go down so it is what you do when you are in office that matters". (Extract from the governor's speech to the South-South governors and National Assembly members' forum, Dec. 7, 2001 in Asaba).

"Our faith in the nation as a federation, where the federating states will have and exercise a reasonable measure of autonomy over their respective resources and contribute to the Federal Government for common services as a whole for the good of present and future generations remains unshaken.

This vision is our article of faith and will be prosecuted with vigor in us for the sake of justice in the exploitation and

*use of the natural resources of the State".
(Extract from the statement by Chief
James Ibori following the judgment of the
Supreme Court in the case of Attorney-
General of the Federation against the
Attorneys-General of 36 states of the
federation published in Vanguard, 24th
April 2002).*

Chief Victor Attah (former Governor Akwa-Ibom State 1999-2007):

*"Please let the impression not be given
that, after we had formed ourselves into the
matrix that binds the belligerent majority
tribes of Nigeria into one country, the only
reason that we are wanted in the union is
so that we can be raped and all our
resources carted away in a manner that
even the worst external colonialist could
not have contemplated.*

*...If we accept this injustice today, what
will be our fate tomorrow? Such diabolical
thing could only be contemplated in a
situation in which the minority has no
rights. Indeed it is yet midnight in the Niger
Delta.*

*...God cannot allow this injustice to
stand against a people who had suffered
so much to keep this country one and who
are now contributing so much from their
God-given resources for the prosperity,
nay survival of this country". (The*

governor reacting to the Supreme Court judgment on the offshore/onshore dichotomy case, Thisday,

Hon. Temi Harriman:

"We from the South-South are begging the North so that we can reach their level. Our place is supposed to be some Mecca of sort. We are not talking of surpassing them in riches. We are saying they should be fair to us to reach normal level with them. Through this, the problem of deprivation and degradation in our areas can be addressed because time is running out. We don't have time. Forget even the psychological damage. What about the restive youths? It is a time bomb. We are not doing this out of selfish reasons. When I go back to my constituency, I feel the heat. How many people can you help personally? We have to do something holistic. This is time for serious and concerted effort" (the honorable in an interview with the Guardian June 25, 2001 after her proposed amendment to the petroleum act failed).

Prof. Itse Sagay:

"The struggle for resource control therefore is not merely one for increased revenue, from the proceeds of one's resources, but more importantly, it is a move by the people of Niger Delta to take their destinies into their own hands. This is

in order to ensure the environmental protection and restoration of the Niger Delta territory to a productive and living one and to insist on environmentally friendly and best oil field practice in the oil and gas extraction process. It is a programme to work for the reinvestment of proceeds of petroleum sales in infrastructure development, environmentally sensitive industries, and in agriculture and aquaculture. It is a campaign for the reforestation, renewal, detoxification and restoration of the land and water of the Niger Delta and the introduction and development of renewable resources. Thus resource control has part of its primary objective, how to ensure life and a good livelihood for the people of the Niger Delta, long after the exhaustion of its petroleum reserves, which have become its enemies" (Federalism, the constitution and resource control: My response by Professor Itse Sagay, published in the Guardian, Monday, August 13, 2003).

Governor Bola Ahmed Tinubu:

While the agitation for SNC initially led by the West part of the country seems to be dying down, Governor Bola Tinubu had propped it up even though we no longer see this agitation, having got lost in the political schemes of the ruling class and himself become a national leader in his party APC, which has nothing of such as its agenda. He was true to the course that brought him to the helms of affairs in Lagos State. Governor Tinubu was among those who ran away from the country in the wake of June 12 crises that almost engulfed the nation. He had joined the growing list of those that the system must take care of in order to kill the agitation.

He came back into the country and was duly elected by the people on the merit of being one that would truly represent their aspirations. The governor while in office continued in this aspiration and did not waver in his unshaken believe in SNC. Like so many that derailed after getting into public offices, Governor Tinubu stood against the system and decried every injustice in it.

He has also kept alive, the memory of those that died in the struggle for June 12 which was the genesis of present democracy. He had immortalized the memory of the martyrs of the struggle. But for him, the struggle would have been confined to the memory of dustbin in the official annals of Nigeria. The fact remains that June 12 brought out the inadequacy in the system and Tinubu kept this alive above everyone else. A vehement critic of the Jonathan Conference, now the party he built and nudged to power, APC are at the helms of affairs, though Tinubu no longer agitates for SNC but he is worth mentioning and hope he will also nudge this party to convoke a true Sovereign National Conference.

The Guardian, Vanguard and Thisday Newspapers

These three newspapers have contributed immensely to the battle for SNC and resource control. The three more than any other papers in the country have given publicity and columns to articles inches to the effect. These have also contributed immensely in granting interviews to persons contributing to the battle for resource control.

Their role in the total emancipation of the Nigerian masses is commendable. They have been very objective in the issues handling. The Guardian must be commended especially after the June 12 battle for which it survived siege of the military. The battle for SNC and resource control still rages and these must keep giving vent to the struggle until the people are liberated from internal colonialism and black man's imperialism.

Ethnic Organizations/Militias:

The state of the nation in the last twenty years, under the various military administrations had led to the frustration of the masses. These bodies had become violent and interested only in the protection of their regional interest. This had led to various inter ethnic clashes where ethnic distrust had continued to be on the rise. The injustice perpetrated within the Nigeria contraption has made the masses of the nation a disoriented people without a slight interest in what the government is doing.

Moreover, the Nigeria masses have little or no faith in the Nigeria nation and so have taken solace in regional cultural organizations that seem to protect their interest. As at late nineties, that is after the June 12 debacle, various organizations had risen to fight the northern oligarchy and the military hold on the nation polity. Prominent among these were the Afenifere, Oodua People's Congress, Movement for the Survival of Ogoni People, Ijaw National Congress, Egbesu and so on.

Most prominent among these were the Afenifere and OPC as well as the Ijaw National Congress. Afenifere, led by Pa Abraham Adesanya easily led the pack in the agitation for an equitable federation within the Nigeria nation, the Ijaw National Congress also led the agitation for total resource control a programme first pushed by the Ken Saro-Wiwa led MOSOP.

In 1998, at an Ibadan summit, held at Laffia Hotel, Afenifere took the military leaders to task by demanding among other things:

- Nigeria should be made into federating units of six regions.
- Decentralization of the military command into regional commands.
- Regional police
- Resource from each region should be control by the producing region while a determined proportion is made to the centre.
- Convocation of sovereign national conference to address the national.

THE RISE OF INSURGENTS

The last insurgent group in the life of the country was the Isaac Adaka Boro insurgency in the sixties. However, in the current dispensation, especially since the current democratic period, the nation has seen the rise of various insurgent groups especially from the Niger Delta and the Northern part of the country. Prominent among these groups are Movement for the Emancipation of the Niger Delta (MEND) and the Boko Haram.

These two tribal insurgent groups can be seen as the symbol of the present Nigerian state and agitation. Both groups have reasons they have decided to take up arms against the system. While the Boko Haram group want a state or nation for themselves guarded by the ideals of Islamism. They want a system that Sharia rules, therefore anything contrary to that is an abomination.

On the other hand MEND wanted a nation where the ethnic nationalities control their resources and decide what to contribute to the union that binds us together. For these two courses several lives have been lost, some have been wasted by these agitators while others were wasted by the government in trying to quell these agitations.

The truth of course is that if the nation does not do something now and drastically, the nation may be plunged into a full blown guerrilla warfare, meaning that for years the nation may become uninhabitable and ungovernable just like Somalia.

The rise of these two militant organizations especially that of Boko Haram can be attributed to the signs of a failed state in which, a people have lost the hope of a better tomorrow. The youths who engaged in Boko Haram rose against education as practiced by the state, this smack of years of neglect of the people by the leaders that govern them. If the ninety percent of the youths in the North Eastern part of the country have been properly educated by the system from independence they would not become foot soldiers for destructive tendencies. Likewise if the nation is working like it should, a militant organization like MEND would not appeal to the youths of the Niger-Delta.

These two organizations may have been contained by the system in the short run which is the usual Nigeria way of doing things, - thinking only in the short term as long as it is beneficial to the leaders and their cronies. However, there will always remain as long as we do not do the right thing, another Boko Haram, another MEND and other ethnic militias, even more in the future until that question which has been since independence and will continue to be until there is an answer **"Why and on what basis must we live together as a nation?"**

The present crops of leaders have gone silent on agitation for SNC and resource control for obvious reasons. For most south westerners, they are now involved in running the affairs of the nation that the goal is no longer the focus. They are too engulfed in politicking to think of SNC. And for the Niger Delta, when a son of the region became the president of the federation, all hostility and agitations were put on hold. The agitation was temporarily put on hold.

None of these augurs well for the struggle as no one is left in the agitation for the struggle to control the anomaly inherent in the configuration of the foundation of this nation. They are involved in the massive looting and the corruption that has pervaded this nation since the new democratic experiment that they are no longer interested in these agitations.

However, the nation groan under the yoke of measures of enslavement, the Niger Delta groan under the weight of overburdened responsibility of having to feed the lust of the corrupt politicians and provide for the development of other parts of the nation's economy. Billions of petrol-naira are looted by the nation's leaders year in year out with no commensurate development in the Niger-Delta or the nation as a whole.

So many agitators for this course have become former champions and are now foot soldiers of the very system which they sought to change. These former vocal chords of SNC and resource control have made us understand that the agitation was only a spring board for them to achieve political relevance. Once they got into political offices, they become the system; they are lost in the system and their agitation become irrelevant as they become antagonists of the very agitation for which they gained recognition.

CHAPTER FIFTEEN

<u>THAT NIGERIA MAY SURVIVE</u>

Having seen the activities of both Boko Haram and MEND, it is clear that this nation is in great turmoil. It is time Nigerians sat down and proffer political solution to the myriad of problems that the leadership seems to be shying away from. The attitude of Nigerians leaders who align themselves with the masses to achieve their political ambitions only to abandon them when they become leaders must stop. Nigerian leaders are great sympathizers of the masses as long as they want political office only to alienate themselves from these same masses as soon as they achieve their personal goals.

For very long, the nation has drifted more to the path of retrogression than to the path of progress. The leaders have not helped matters. While the nation wallows in poverty and the Niger Delta under the yoke of enslavement, billions of the nation's loots are stashed away in foreign land to boost such economies. The leaders have displayed short-sightedness in economic matters. They have become amateurs in handling political issues. They have displayed cowardice in matters affecting the nation. While leaders from the North cannot be blamed, the same cannot be said of the Southern leaders who have in the face intimidation chickened out of just struggles.

This political class plays the script of their feudal employers as soon as they found themselves in the positions of power. The survival of the nation has become the survival of their pockets. Common weal has become personal and pocket weal. A nation that has abandon justice and equal rights for its people, which has played the card of ethnicity, religion and favoritism, will soon collapse.

The leaders yet believe they have the real interest of the nation at heart. They are the lords of the masses and their thoughts only could be good for the people. Whatever measures they designed, the people must like morons tow the line. The people are like the cows of the nomadic herdsman who must whip his cows to fall into line.

The survival of the nation is not as paramount in the minds of the leaders as it is in the mind of every crusader of SNC and resource control. But the fact remains that for Nigeria to survive there must be fairness and justice within the nation polity. It is this fairness that will translate to good fortune for every citizen but as it is most Nigerians have lost faith in the nation called Nigeria and the leaders know this fact. Ex-Governor Achike Udenwa of Imo State admitted this much in his speech to the other Southern governors in his domain. He said inter alia:

> *"My brother governors, I stand before you today as one of you, truly concerned about, and patriotically committed to, the indivisibility of this great nation. All of us are agreed on this, which explains why we are relentless in our search for true federation. Yet you must permit me to agitate your minds a while on the symbol of our unity.*
>
> *How many ordinary Nigerians do you think have genuine faith in their country? How*

many ordinary Nigerians do you think believe that they can get justice from their country? How many ordinary Nigerians do you think believe they can get protection from their country? The list of question is endless but I believe you and I know the answers. What the answers you get from your heart's mind tell you is a big contraption that needs urgent surgery.

As leaders, we cannot and should not run away from this sad reality. Let me therefore enjoin this August summit to rise from this meeting with a clear reiteration of our insistence on a true federation as the only way forward for our fatherland.

A true federation should allow all the federating units to determine their destiny. A true federation should allow the federating units to control their resources. A true federation should allow the federating units to promote and practice their religious beliefs to the best of their desire but not at the detriment of that of others. We cannot hope to make any meaningful progress if we insist on imposing the present unifederal contraption on our people. As leaders, we must face the inevitable sooner or later.

Posterity will not forgive those whose lot it will be to be used as willing tools to traumatize the collective desire of our peoples. That desire is a true and free federation where the nation shall provide an unfettered environment for peace, justice, security and the right for individual and group to self-actualization. Our people desire a nation where the instrument of state is not seen as an agent for the exploitation of the wealth of the weak for the well being of the strong. They expect a nation where both the weak and the strong shall coexist as equal partners in progress, drawing protection from that inexhaustible divine fountain from whence flow the ageless inalienable rights of man: freedom, justice and equity" (Speech by Gov. Achike Udenwa of Imo State at the 5th Summit of Southern Governors' Conference in Owerri, November 2001).

The unity of Nigeria cannot be compromised by any one ethnic nationality, be it the Yorubas, the Ibos, the Hausas, Ijaws, Urhobos, Ogonis etc. Nigeria as a political unit cannot be compromised, at least not after the Ibos had been so wasted in a nation that had no regard for decorum and respect for the lives of its citizens. Too much has gone into building Nigeria into one unit for anyone group to jeopardize its unity. However, Nigeria cannot be united in diversity.

There can be nothing like unity in diversity; this has been too long a deceptive phrase that has been used when the big brothers knew the only unity in the country is the soul of the Niger Delta. Unity is accepting our differences first. Then we sit to discuss these differences. The differences in particular groups will be used to develop the individual group. Then we shall recognize our common grounds and develop the common grounds as a nation and as one people. This will be done with mutual respect and bond to the new union as negotiated by the ethnic nationalities.

The unique difference in our Nigerianness must be made clear and these differences must be the basis upon which we base our desire to live together as one nation. When this is done, then the nation is ready for the future. The contribution of each to the nation must be based only on common features that bind us together mutually and it is in this that we build the nation that we want. Thus the Hausa is equal to the Kanuri, the Kanuri equal to the Jukun, the Jukun equal to the Ibiobio. The Ibiobio equal to the Ogoni, the Ogoni equal to the Ijaw, the Ijaw equal to the Itshekiri, the Itshekiri equal to the Urhobo, the Urhobo equal to the Edo, the Edo equal to the Yoruba and all equal one nation within the central policy.

When a system is unfair, tyrannical and oppressive, then the people must be ready for a rising up against it. This is not a rising up against the North. It is not a rising up against any group or against individual. It is a rising up against the system. It is a rising up against a system that has turned a section of its citizens into second class citizens. It is a rising against a system that plundered a people's legacy to leave them impoverished. A system that encourages mediocrity against hard work must be done away with. A system that promotes ingenuity against genuine aspirations is moribund. A system that guarantees no security for its citizen, a system that kills the people's desire for self-actualization, a system that cares not for the future of the citizens, a system so averse to changes, this is the system that must be replaced.

This is not about tongue, neither is it about religion, nor is it about ethnicity, it is about justice. It is about a people's legacy. It is about the future of an entire generation, about a people's resolve to remain one. It is about Nigeria. So that Nigeria may survive. Sovereign National Conference denies no one his sovereign power. So why be afraid of it? If truly the leaders are not just bunch of power hungry individuals whose only concern is how to hold on to power, then now is the time to prove their mettle and set the nation on the right path for true greatness.

SNC will only guard against the future of everyone within the nation and ensure that we indeed answer the questions on the basis of our coexistence. This is the yearning of the masses. This is the same yearning that the leaders have capitalized on to rise to political prominence within their constituencies. It is the same yearning that the feudal lords have sought to kill using the bait ethnicity and religion. They do not feel it, only the masses do. This is because they are the suffering lots. They are the pawns in this game. That is why they have to vote when called upon. They welcome the military that set the nation on the path of retrogression. They allowed the trial of their patience and accept their lots. That patience is far expended. The leaders must make haste to correct the wrongs of amalgamation. They must right the wrongs of years of plunder within the nation as a whole and the Niger Delta in particular.

SNC will not threaten the basis of our coexistence nor will resource control create inequalities in the nation. Resource control will rather create a healthy competition among the federating units. Nigeria has suddenly abandoned its potential. We have started chasing shadows. Over-dependence on the oil in the Niger Delta is creating greater inequalities within the nation.

SNC and resource-control do not call for the division of the nation. It makes bold to strengthen it. What it proposes is a replacement of the system with a stronger. It proposes a replacement with one that guarantees protection from abuse and frees all from the shackles of this internal neo-colonialism of blacks on blacks. Those scared of these are the slots in the system, those who know on their own merit, they would be nowhere. Those scared that their means of free wealth will be taken away. They are those who have amassed wealth from the soul of the nation without a drop of their own sweat. They are the beneficiaries of present system's injustice; they are the favored ones and would stop at nothing to maintain the status quo.

Those who are scared of SNC are the ones who do not want to be told the truth, the truth that Nigeria was a contraption of different ethnic nationalities that had lived as independent political entities before the forceful acquisition of the territories by the Europeans and the forceful amalgamation of the North and South must be accepted. SNC is meant to bring us closer to our history, from which we seem to have drifted. The SNC is a means to begin rebuilding from the foundation, to spell out the terms of our coexistence so that we can live together in peace and not in pieces always tearing at each other. It is meant to develop mutual respect from every Nigerian to another.

It is meant to bring back the faith in Nigeria, which of course, had never been there. It is meant to give security and safety to everyone irrespective of one's tribe, religion or place of residence within the nation. SNC is meant to educate us further on what we were before the colonialists came. It is meant to tell us how much we have derailed, where we are presently, where we ought to be, and where we want to be. It will help us spell out how we will be there. It is meant to tell us how we ought to live as one and equal people not as conquered entities living in a neo-colonial era.

Every ethnic nationality will then pledge their abiding faith to the new union knowing it is a contract of the people by the people, made by the people for the survival of the nation, the protection of the union and the glory of our fatherland - NIGERIA. This will form the basis of interaction between the future generations of Nigerians. It will build a definite pattern of nation building and not the erratic demonstration of madness that we have experienced in our almost one century of existence as a contraption. The future is now to be decided, Nigeria cannot be negotiated away, and it must survive.

As it is right now, the Nigeria of our dream has remained only in our dream in a dreamland. Present leadership is never waking up to the challenges presented by the fact that it is made up of different systems that only connects mutually end-to-end but working independently to sustain the entire body. This is the reality to be faced. This is the reality on ground. Nigerians must seat down to decide and strengthen that point that connects end to end while not neglecting the cells that hold the end-to-end points.

This must be done while the cells work independently to keep the entire system in place. This must be the guiding philosophy. This should be the Nigerian contract, not chains of fanciful dreams in the imaginations of some lunatic leader intoxicated and dazzled by the liquor of power. The leaders must wake up from the illusive dreams of a united Nigeria tied only at the apron string of active volcanic crater waiting for time to erupt. It is the end-to-end cell connections that must work to keep the nation one.

SNC and resource-control are not divisive tendencies, they are meant to give the Nigerian a pride of place in the union. They are meant to secure the future of the hardworking Nigerian so that he or she can attain self actualization, reach full potential and contribute positively to the development of Nigeria. It is meant to make the centre less attractive for political jobbers, whose only goal is the looting of the nation's treasury. We must aim to bring forth men with true nationalistic spirit to lead the nation.

Nigeria should not be an empire permanently subordinate to any one section of the country. A mutual agreement has to be made and it is only an SNC that can ensure that. This is because; the draft will be superior to any other document in the nation history. Pertinent issues must be resolved an like John Hatch (1970) questioned, we have to determine:

- How hostile rival societies live together under one administration peacefully without trampling on the rights of the other?
- How do we create a single nation devoid of ethnic rancor?
- How do we avoid undue dominance of the polity by a single region, tribe or religion to the

detriment of the others be they minorities or majority?

- How do we develop competitive, thrusting and dynamic society where all individuals are given equal opportunities to develop themselves and contribute positively to build a virile and united nation?

- How do we incorporate our youths into nation building rather than allow them waste in the current vices of cultism, religious bigotry, ethnic militias and armed robbery thereby endangering their future?

- How do we compensate the old who have dedicated themselves to nation building in their youths and take care of the less privileged, the handicapped without sending them into the streets as beggars?

- What legacies do we bequeath for the future knowing the past has been squandered?

- How do we prevent the looting of the nation's resources by greedy Nigerian leaders and also prevent the squandering of the resources on non-visible developments?

- Most of all how do we ensure that the national polity is never hijacked by some trigger happy Nigerians sustained by the tax of hardworking   Nigerians   under
flimsy excuses of patriotism?

These are issues that must be ironed out. It is not democracy; democracy cannot answer the questions above, that the country – Nigeria may survive; these questions/issues need to be ironed out once and for. Democracy is not the answer to them; it is only the peaceful means through which the process can be achieved. These issues transcend democracy, tribe, and religion. Only a conference of ethnic nationalities can iron them out. The original thirteen states of the U.S. negotiated their union. Canada negotiated.

Yugoslavia did not agree to sit and negotiate, USSR ran the other nations in it as conquered communist's territories, but today neither USSR nor Yugoslavia is on the world map, which is after about seventy years. Europe is negotiating their unity so why not Nigeria? The British Empire that bundled us together against our wish asked the people of \Northern Ireland to decide on their own if they wanted to remain part of Britain or attain self determination, the countries in the Union of United Kingdom have a working term. Ethiopia could not keep Eritrea, Burundi almost collapsed until they negotiated. The nations waxing very strong today are the ones with clear-cut definition of the basis for national unity. Democracy is not the optional replacement for SNC and resource control. It is only a stepping stone to the peaceful attainment of the goals of these two struggles or else it is an unnecessary gerrymandering and a moving in an endless circle of confusion.

Nigeria is not searching for options in democracy, as this would not solve the problems. It is a game of winner takes it all. The weak will thus never be protected; the minority will only be forced to tag along without

238

being part of the system. If not for special arrangement, the result of the 1999 elections would have been different. And if Bola Ige had not died, the result of the 2003 elections would still not have been different. Nigeria will return to the old order and the problems persist.

The majority tribes will lead and the minority tribes will remain in perpetual slavery. The minorities will be the basis of the unity of the major tribes, or else; they would have nothing to gain in the contraption called Nigeria. The system is better discarded and fast before the basis of national unity become less attractive to all and the nation heads for the brink of collapse. Then it would be too late to salvage. The SNC is to save the Niger Delta and their resources.

The present clamor for resource control should therefore go with the clamor for an SNC. The Niger Deltan is not just entitled to her resources; she also has the right to aspire to lead the nation. It is the SNC that will ensure that her rights are never again trampled upon and she is never treated as slave by the Federal Government or all other ethnic nationalities, be they major or minor, the Oil companies, and by the other ethnic groups within the nation. This will also ensure that her future is guaranteed within the nation.

This is indeed a battle for the soul of the Niger Delta as it is time for the region to take its destiny in her arm. The nation must acknowledge the bridging role that the region had played and duly give its due to it. The plunder must stop now, the enslavement brought to an end, imperial practice of the oil companies stopped and the people allowed freedom to determine their own destinies because like Honorable Temi Harriman rightly put it:

"Within another 30 to 40 years, according to experts, the oil will be finishing. Meaning the Niger Delta is sinking, the ocean is coming in, the land is going down, even underneath, the land, it all potholes. We don't even know what is going to happen; whether there is going to be an earthquake we don't know.

That oil is not going to be there in the next generation. So what we are saying is that if you have an educated workforce today with necessary structures on ground, we should bequeath something to our people. If we have an industrial hub in this area, we would have bequeathed something. We are not saying we are not ready to share. After all, they said they had groundnut, cocoa, and palm oil. We are saying ours is not agricultural resources like theirs. We are saying the land is sinking and the asset in our land is wasting. Recently, experts' reports had it that we are 75% worse off in Nigeria in spite of our oil wealth over the years. All the money made from oil has been squandered on white elephant projects by our leaders, we are poorer today than before we found oil almost 40 years ago". (The Guardian, Tuesday 5, 2001).

The people of the Niger Delta must realize the enormous power at their disposal right now:

- Having the economic advantage of negotiation, which is a major rule of crisis prevention?
- Having abundant human resources and control of the nation's bulk of press.
- The fact that every other ethnic nationality feel aggrieved with the system.
- Now is the time to negotiate a better deal for the restructuring of the federation.

The relevance of Niger Delta within the entity called Nigeria must right now be emphasized. The stigma of a restive people needing special attention must be erased. The Niger Delta cannot be relevant to the politics of the nation only because it feeds the rest of the country. The time has now come for the people to be actively involved in the politics of the nation. This is the time. The Niger Delta can now negotiate with the rest of the nation because it is at an advantage position. If this chance passes by then we are doomed to remain slaves to rest of the nation forever.

It must be engraved in the heart of the other ethnic nationalities that the region holds the key to national unity. The rest of the nation must be made to realize that the name of the country was derived from the region and as such the people must be shown some measure of respect. The people must rise to the occasion to earn this respect for themselves. It is time that this plunder must cease.

Now that the region is the wielding block of the nation, for the rest of the ethnic groups all agree that their basis of coexistence within the Nigeria contraption is the politics of crude oil found within the Niger Delta region. If the wells run dry then there is no basis for the existence of the Nigeria nation. The leaders must now be awake to their responsibilities, a duty they owe the people, to negotiate for them, a greater participation in the politics of the nation and greater participation in the control of the resources of the Niger Delta.

For too long, other ethnic nationalities have decided the destiny and played politics with the future of the people of the region, the time has come that the people must come together as one, speaking with one voice to decide for themselves, a new course. This is the duty that the leaders must rise up to. It is time to call the bluff of a system that has continually plundered and squandered the people's legacy. This is so that the future of the people might be guaranteed for only the people have the right to decide their own destiny, for long this destiny has been decided by strangers who are the joyful vultures that have invaded the land and plunder its resources. And like the late Victor Hugo said:

"Nothing can stop an idea whose time has come"

And like Fidel Castro also said

"Ideas do not generate crisis, crisis generate ideas"

The crisis within the nation must be resolved, enough of the pretence that all is well while the masses especially the Niger Delta people groan in the yoke of slavery.

APPENDIX

<h1 style="text-align:center"><u>APPENDIX I:</u></h1>

<u>DANCE OF THE PEACOCK</u>

By VICTOR DENILA

Creation radiated beauty
The glory of the creator in it shone
The blue sea was beautiful
The trees in the thick forest
The birds that sang so happily
All the animals in the forest
The eyes of him that created beheld
Behold all things were good
Man was created, the crown of creation
The perfection of all things seen and unseen
In eternal illumination
Covered in unmerited glory
The envy of angelic beings
On the altar of perfection
Devotion to the grail so chaste
All at corner, a looming darkness
Upon creation
An invasion from Hades
Of damned incubi
Warned but unguarded
Blinded with lust
Lewd angels of hell
Casting lecherous glances at the fruit
Ways of perversion suddenly turned
Sudden gloom upon creation
Yet in gloomy pride he swung
Celebrating peacockic vanity
Pride lost never to regain

Now basking in peacockic glory
The peacock in color of vanity
Graceful steps of emptiness
Popped up from within
Beauty so exaggerated
Casting lustful desires
As snare for them that falls
A dance so embraced
The peacock rules the floor
Howling and bullying
Creation to panic

Yet in his nothingness they marveled
Sycophants to the stage
A drama of mockery
This voice, the peacock, discern not
Dance of the peacock
A dance to the deception of men
Hawks in flirtatious moves
The eagles silenced
The dove ramshackle
Falcons in deep slumber
Dance, dance, dance, the peacock dance
Laugh, laugh, laugh, they laughed
For him they marvel
Idolized sycophancy
The peacock in clownish dance
Undescerned fallen glory
Creation has fallen, tell the peacock
There is no grace in the dance
The luster is faded
Why dance the peacock still
Glowing in vulturic holiness
Basking in parrotic sycophancy
Blinded to dovic subtlety

Little starling to the fore
To sing discordant melody
Ego-boosting tune for his desires
This dance of ignoble pride
Which only self beauty accord
Stop the noise of the starling
Bring back the days of the nightingale
When the eagle in full strength swung
The falcon winked not in slumber
The dove for peace and justice stood
Then all our wealth of beauty
Which the peacock on himself adorned
All shall beautify
This dance to an end must come
So the ruin rebuilt
And the master Artist
Mortals shall exonerate
Of a fault in a bid
For self will to be
Which to cannibalism led

Man in endless search
For the preternatural path
The deceptive ways of the hood
Basking in hyper-natural blindness
The tears of unfulfilled lusts
With hard pangs creation held
Groan with desires
For the milk of freedom
Yet in endless gerrymandering
Popped up in peacockic pride
Distorting the natural arrangement
Ever in fear of the shadows
Seeking perfection
Which only from the mouth of sycophants come

In display of vulturic tendencies
Attuned to parrotic psyche
And the graceful steps of the peacock
In love of the pseudo-messiah
Devising only means of strangulation
Leading generations to ruin
Averse to the ways of nature
Perversion of the Holy Grail
Hood-cooked bondage
Souls for eternal damnation
Lewd sons of hell
In dance of deception
Mastered by the peacock
Tutored by the vulture
Ego-tripped by the starling
On the altar of collapse
A fall that came ere the pride
One step dance of the peacock
Eternal bang the order
Effete, yet total confusion
A search so futile
For an undiscovered shadow
That to hell leads
Yet never ready faults to accept
Perverted puritans
With veiled perceptions
Reprobate dance of the peacock
To an end shall come one day

In torrent of mental derangement
Cackling away, valuable time
Lost in the ocean of nothingness
Clownic manifestation of inner rumbling
Peace upon creation such gold
Romance with demons in a defiled matrimony

Frantic search for the eagle
A plea for the return of the dove
So the dance of the peacock
To a lull might go
Only in a new form to re-launch
Aided by subtle machinations
Enthroned by abominable reprobates
All souls to fate resigned
In anticipation of the millennia
Even nature groans
From the weight if its sapped enthalpy
Crises of ideals
Conflicts of idiosyncrasies
Never man to correct
But immutable things to replace
Even at the turn of the messiah
Little imps to the stage came
The vision to impair
The hope to kill
Then all over begins again
The search for the paradise of time
Another maneuver of the peacock
Embers of dead ego to fan
Mendicants all souls become
Pauperized so in chains can remain
And this dance of deception
On and on goes
For the overbearing sons of perdition
Peregrination into cataclysmic epoch
And mortals with modicum faith
In joy of the new experience
From which the peacockic ghouls
Forever cast away
And the dance of the peacock
Forever ceased.

In anticipation of the millenic age
An age of obstinate serenity
Yet mortals not the faintest perception
Of the lurking catastrophe
That a new Stone Age ushered
A total cleansing of
A gerrymandering age of peacockic deceptions
Souls in demonic procession
The undertakers' field day
Vultures in East of corpses
Feeding fat upon the spoils
Of ignoble peacockic dance
Which the wrath of the gods brought
Upon the battle of harvest
The Harvester comes to the reaping
The husband-man in joy of
Bountiful harvest
Which his labor brought
Fear no more of lurking
Messengers of Hades
Whose plague tears brought
The dance of the peacock
No more attraction shall be
Transmogrified souls
The new earth to inhabit
Dressed and prepared by the master Artist
Without a fault
Men of modicum faith
And a panting desire
Which this new city seek
Insatiable souls of peacockic age
That like the eagle found their strength
Like the dove make peace
Like the falcon watch in anticipation
250

Which shadows of pains endure
Shall be rested in the bosoms
Of eternal illumination
Which in the age shall light mortals
Whose souls groaned in the
Awful dance of the peacock
That eternal damnation brought
Overthrown by pride of his beauty
An outcast eternally.

APPENDIX II:

NUDITY
By VICTOR DENILA

The full moon
Upon the raffia roof
The tinny paths
To my *'ogede'* farms
The thatched fences
Loved by the *'alamgbas'*
In my nudity
Serenity upon the mother earth
To the rivers' goddess *'olokun'*
Serenity unequalled

In my childish whims
The earth so whimsical
Illusory day-dreams of a chaste mind
The sky so ethereal
Of my innocent dreams
Hopes no longer can give
In my nudity
To mother earth I look
So discomforted
Mother earth my being comforted

Turbulence upon my soul
Destruction upon my body
Vicissitude upon my essence
My nudity
Mama no longer there, to cover
Upon my skull
Thunderous ache

Upon my heart
Pangs of sadness
My soul aches for serenity

My nudity who will cover
In my bowels
Monstrous seeds
My head bald with age
My bladders, piss no longer can hold
The scorching sun
My tender skin crack
My nude no one will cover
Who my tears to dry?
Who my yearning to satisfy?

APPENDIX III:

THE EXORCIST
By VICTOR DENILA

The mind, the soul, the body
Daemon to possess
The thrill, the excitement
Frenzy in essence
Splash, splash, splash
Tum, tum, tum, tum
The rare scare of my soul
On a journey to eternity
The rapacious beings
My soul longs to possess
The unconscious rape of my will
Through my anus
Daemons came to possess
My soul, a ramshackle structure
Two destinies, my soul to decide
One destiny, my soul to face
Sky of unknown expanse
Wither my choice?
My essence, this coffin must leave
Daemons, my coffin must depart
The exorcist, my essence
Come liberate
The exorcist, sweet chants
My soul pants
Like the scare of rushing winds
Daemons my soul depart
The serenity of the deep blue sea
My essence filled
One destiny that my soul knows

Upon eternity
The secret of our heart rests
To my exorcist
The transmogrification of my soul
I, thee essence who can hole?
Sanity, back to my soul
Demons forever depart
My exorcist
There by me, you to scare
Our love deified.

APPENDIX IV:

THE JOYFUL VULTURES
By JOSHUA DENILA

Olokun sang
The umpires danced
The throes of Sango
Forever they petted
And hawks came
I was shown the way
To the pot of life
And dominion it had known
From the ageless masters
Facelessly they officiate
The depredations of black soils
Feasting in darkness
And in the vultures' pouch
Gawkily they rambled
Crooning endlessly
In joyful loots
Pinched faces
Beaming smiles of desolation
Their puppets-
Evince stumps of genuine cupidity
O! The joyful vultures
Feeding fat from the cries of black souls
Chortling at stage-managed dreams
Melancholy…despondency…
God would not look on
Lips of judgment must part
Sorrowful corpses must smile
And embrace their generations
To Hades – the gods amongst men

Enough of the vultures' joy
Enough of their offensive mien
A prim judgment must prevail.

APPENDIX V:

YONKS OF SERVITUDE
By JOSHUA DENILA

When the peace of the lagoon is bludgeoned
Its stillness roars their deviance
Nature beckons
The impoverished
The ravished
With tumultuous sleet
In your hands lie the wands
To upturn your destiny
Death to the yonks of servitude
Let subjects sully the king
With a mega-ego
Let his grandeur transmogrify
Into parch air
And his soul
Into parch hell
On his being, paraplegia is wrought
And the land shall become paradisiacal
Cleansed with his blood
Swallowed by a cursed earth
Chains shall quake
Hearts shall no longer thump
Thump with a call
To the messiah
From the yonks of servitude, death
When the vampire is bludgeoned across the Styx
The stillness of the lagoon
Would no longer be altered
The roar of defiance
Will no more be heard.

APPENDIX VI:

MY SOUL IS IN PRISON
By JOSHUA DENILA

Like a miserable brat
At war with life
In a wizened visage
Once I brawl

Fantastic denizens
Splendours souls
With refulgent glories
Succumb to dereliction

My debauchery
I desire no more
To the wind I give
My treachery

Endless hassles
Haunts our three masters
Recklessly abandoning in them
Fragments of shambles

I bleed in the confinement of my soul
Wail, till the death do me harm
When shall the pangs of oppression wane?
Puke! My taste sours

The course of depredation furthered
The hedonist, the sadists, and the despot
Dictate the destinies of men
Oceans of depredations are fathered

Aloof tramping!
Offspring of godly souls
Festooning the cities
With acrimonious caravansary of tramps

In this murk of nothingness we grope
In our emptiness we groan
In our gyp we plead with the monsters
That stare imperiously at our hope

In the hound of death
We wallow oh! Oh! Bleeding
Bleed with muted call to death
Come and take our gyp.

ABOUT THE AUTHOR

Victor Denila was born Sept. 17, 1972 in Ile-Ife, Osun State, he hails from Delta State, Nigeria. He graduated from the University of Lagos with a B.Sc in Geography. He was a students' union activist.

He held various students' union positions while at University of Lagos. Victor Denila is a prolific writer, film producer/director.

THE BATTLE FOR THE SOUL OF NIGER-DELTA

The Niger-Delta is the resource base of Nigeria, yet a lot of injustice seems to be going as the people are deprived and poverty reigns in the region while the ruling class gets richer. This essay examines the basis of the existence of Nigeria as a country and the injustice perpetrated by the ruling class.

It also traces the history of various ethnic nationalities and the need for the overhauling of the entire system that brings the country into existence. While advocating oneness, this oneness must be based on justice and consent of the various ethnic groups defining the basis of their co-existence. This must be done through a sovereign national conference or the overhauling of the present constitution of the federation.